JOHN SCHWARTZKOPF

WORKS 2007-2014

Front cover: *The Wave*
Back cover: *Mosaic Portrait of John Schwartzkopf.* Copyright © 2005, David Van Allen. All rights reserved.

Concrescent Network LLC, publisher.
1113 19th St SE, Cedar Rapids, IA, 52403

ISBN: 978-0-9890238-1-8

JOHN SCHWARTZKOPF

WORKS 2007-2014

CONTENTS

MAKING WOOD DANCE: THE ART OF JOHN SCHWARTZKOPF   6

INTRODUCTION   10

THE WORK: 2007-2014   13

REFLECTIONS ON THE WORK   98

CREDITS AND ACKNOWLEDGMENTS   122

MAKING WOOD DANCE: THE ART OF JOHN SCHWARTZKOPF

The art of John Schwartzkopf is…art. It's just that most people don't think about his work that way. This is due, in part, to how John came to where he is today, through woodworking and the creation of gorgeous yet functional pieces. His benches, sideboards, cabinets, and tables—while beautiful—all have a function to fulfill. This dichotomy, between function and beauty, has colored discussions about beautiful yet functional objects throughout the twentieth century. Through the labors of many important artists in the worlds of glass, metals, ceramics, and wood, there has been a return to the concept that things that are useful can also be beautiful.

John has always adhered to this concept. In fact, his benches are sometimes so beautiful that people are not sure if they are allowed to sit on them.

John has taken his origins in functional art and used them to explore the world of non-functional sculptural art. Here, in discrete three-dimensional works, John has created works which are a natural extension of his functional objects. They retain the same sense of beauty, grace, balance, and compositional harmony that one finds in all great works of art. At the same time, they are a reflection of the artist. Anyone who knows John knows that he is inextricably linked to his creations. The work reflects John and John is clearly in his work. The two are one.

Part of the reason John is at one with his work is that he listens to his materials and they tell him what he needs to know—all he needs to know. In his studio—his shop as he calls it—he lives with the materials and, over time, they reveal themselves to him. As a wood artist, he needs to listen carefully to his material. Wood, unlike other materials, is still alive. It moves, changes, expands and contracts even after the artist has finished his creation. John understands this. He works with the material, not against it. He does what it tells him, not the other way around.

But it's not just wood. John combines natural wood with manmade materials such as PaperStone, Environ, Synskin, and aluminum to create a collage or assemblage of the natural and the fabricated. Ultimately, that's what John is—a collage artist. In the process of creation, John seeks out a perfect harmony between the natural and the manmade—obtaining a delicate balance so that one does not overwhelm the other. In the end, he is satisfied when a graceful relationship is established.

Gracefulness is the underlying quality in all John's work. Whether it is the graceful edge of a piece of wood, or the undulating wood grains within it, or the poetic balance between forms and materials, the result is always a piece that is harmonious. The tension he creates between the linear and the organic, with his use of arcing forms, results in a certain sense of motion. This may be why several works possess titles that speak of motion: tango, dance, rapids, rhythm. It's there. The works are not static—they are moving. Or about to spring into action.

This tension is achieved through a sensitive approach to the form. His work reflects a more minimal sensibility, and possesses all the elegance and formality that comes with that. Such elegant simplicity is reminiscent of earlier artists such as Agnes Martin and Barbara Hepworth, with whom he is a kindred spirit. Also at play is his awareness of Asian culture, especially Asian aesthetics. While this is visible in his resultant works, it can also be found in his use of bamboo and titles referencing pagodas and the samurai. More than anything, the formal elegance of his work bespeaks his Asian inspirations.

At the very root of all of his work is his incredible reverence and respect of nature. Not only is his work largely created out of an element of nature—wood—but natural forces are seen in many of his works. Earth, wind, sky, waves, and the prairie are all at play in this work, and many of his titles reflect those influences. John is keenly attuned to the motions and rhythms of nature and they are ultimately the foundation of all he creates.

Although John might not call himself a great artist—modesty would prevent him—he does create great art. Whether investigating ways to reveal nature's bounty in his functional benches, tables, and sideboards, or the forces of nature in his minimal, elegant, and graceful three-dimensional pieces, John is always true to himself which means he is also true to his muse, nature.

Sean M. Ulmer
Executive Director
Cedar Rapids Museum of Art

INTRODUCTION

This portfolio presents images of work completed between 2007 and 2014. These represent only a sample, intended to represent the range within which I work. These mostly comprise what I think of as *studio work*: projects which are purely conceptual in nature without consideration as to context or placement. They tend to be experimental at times, allowing me to try out new ideas or explore the limits of new materials. Since I have no constraints on the design or size of the piece, it is a good gauge of my current approach to my work.

Commission work, however, comprises a large percentage of my work. This puts constraints on the scale of the work that often require different approaches to a piece than that what I might otherwise take. While these constraints can provide unique opportunities, these projects are informed by ideas forged by the studio work. While this work is only represented here by a couple of examples, including more pieces would not provide more insight into my approach to the work. It would make the book rather unwieldy in scale, so I have put these images on my website instead.

THE WORK: 2007-2014

98H X 43W X 12.5D

Crafted of Cherry, Walnut, and Maple
2014

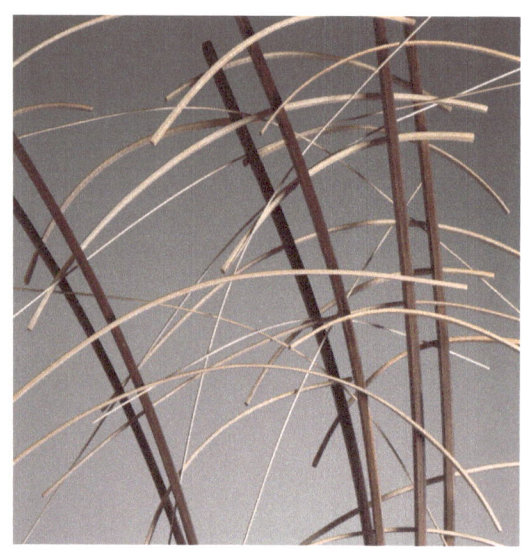

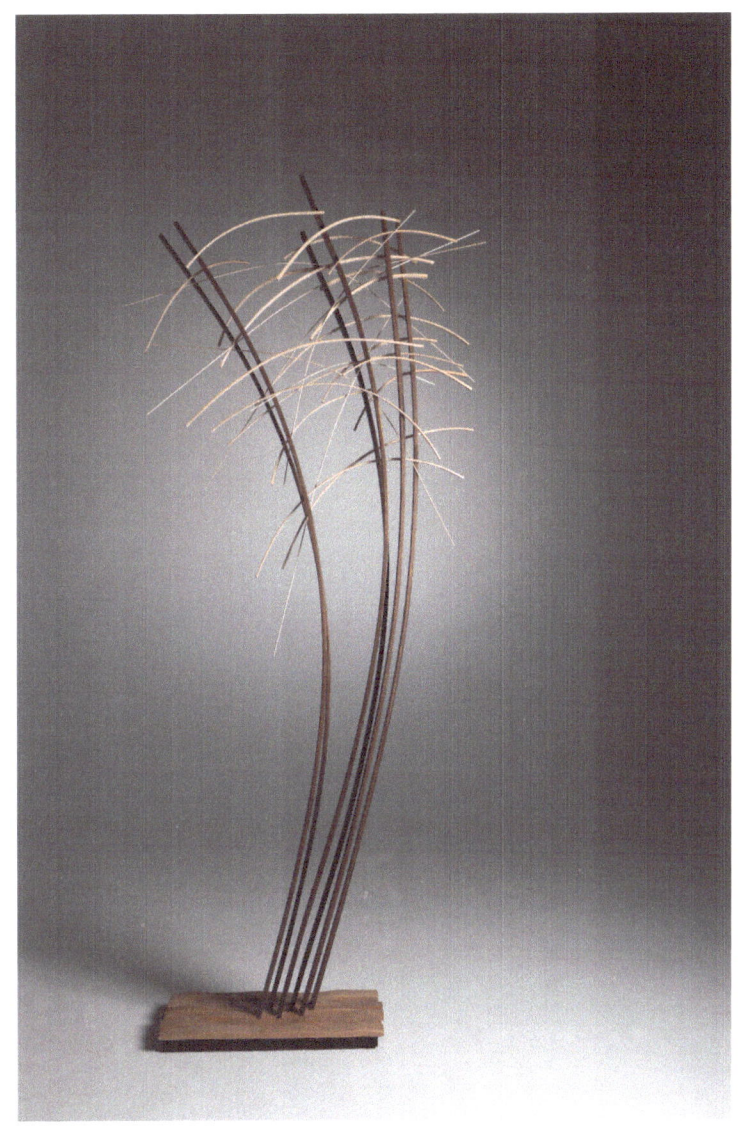

30H x 98W x 9D

Crafted of Maple, Mahogany, and Wenge
2009

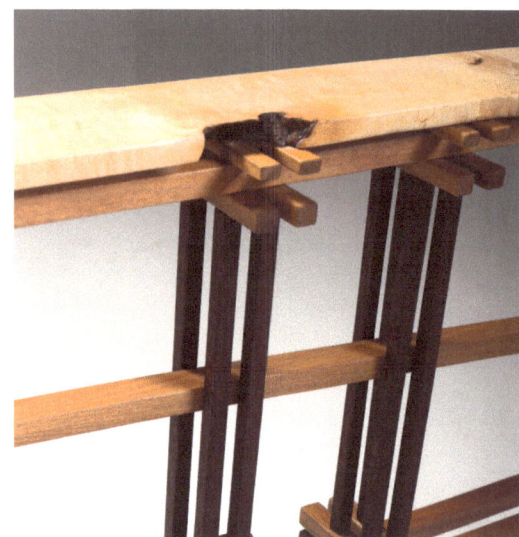

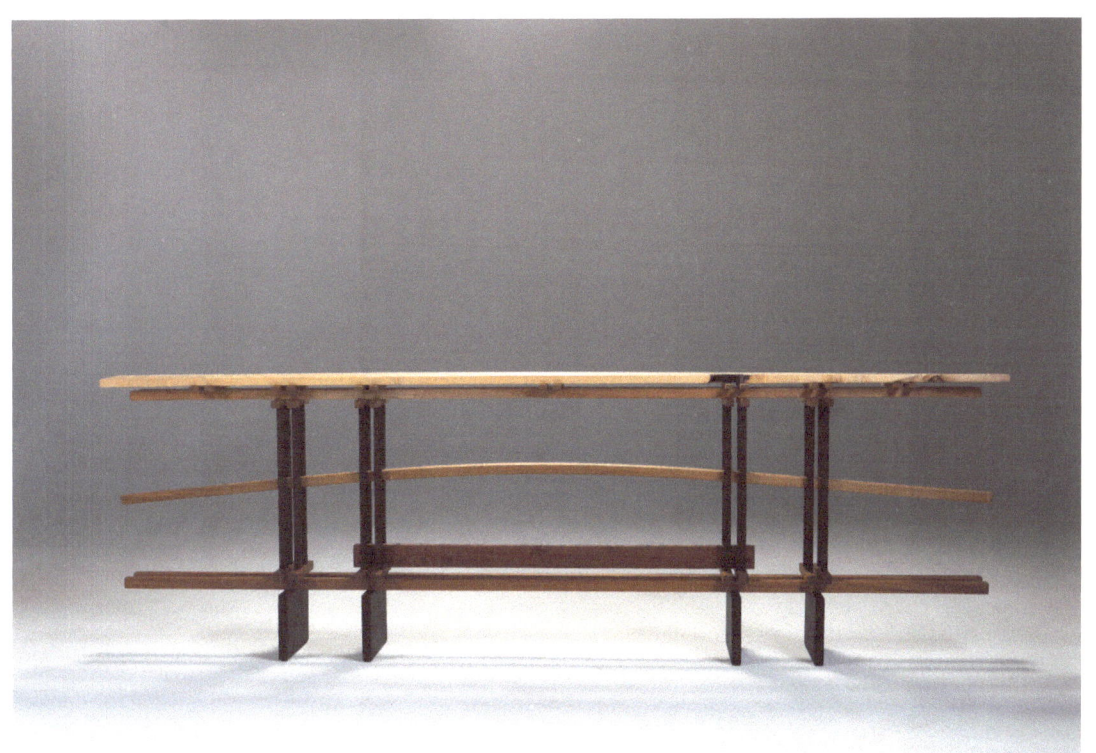

57H X 13W X 8D

Crafted of PaperStone
2009

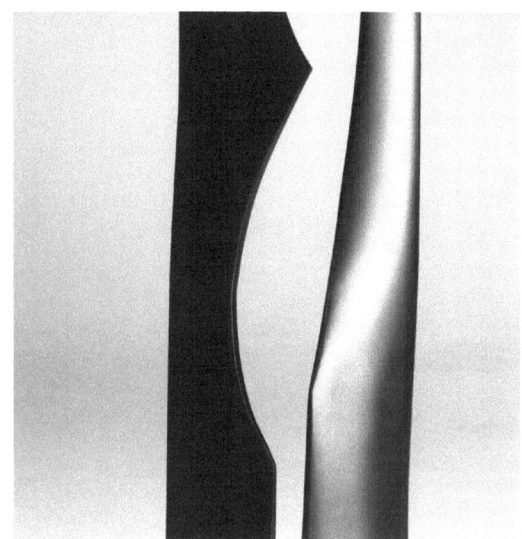

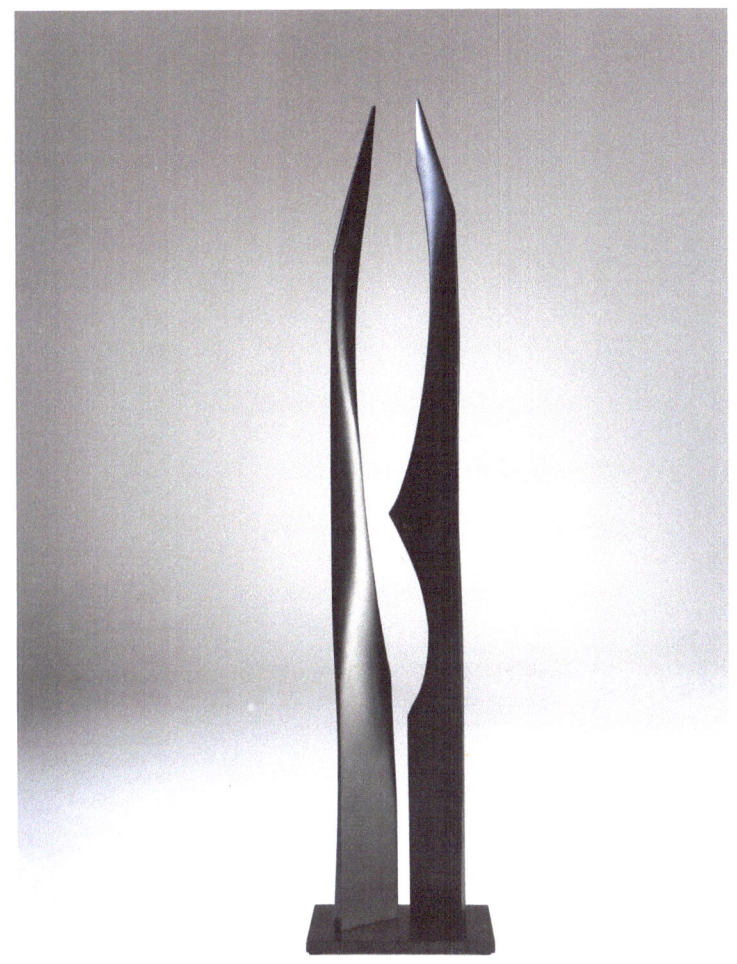

GEOMETRIC TANGO

108H X 20W X 14.5D

Crafted of Bamboo, Maple, and PaperStone
2013

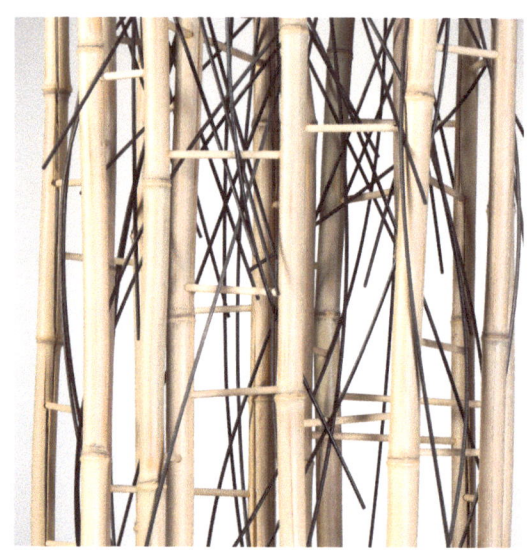

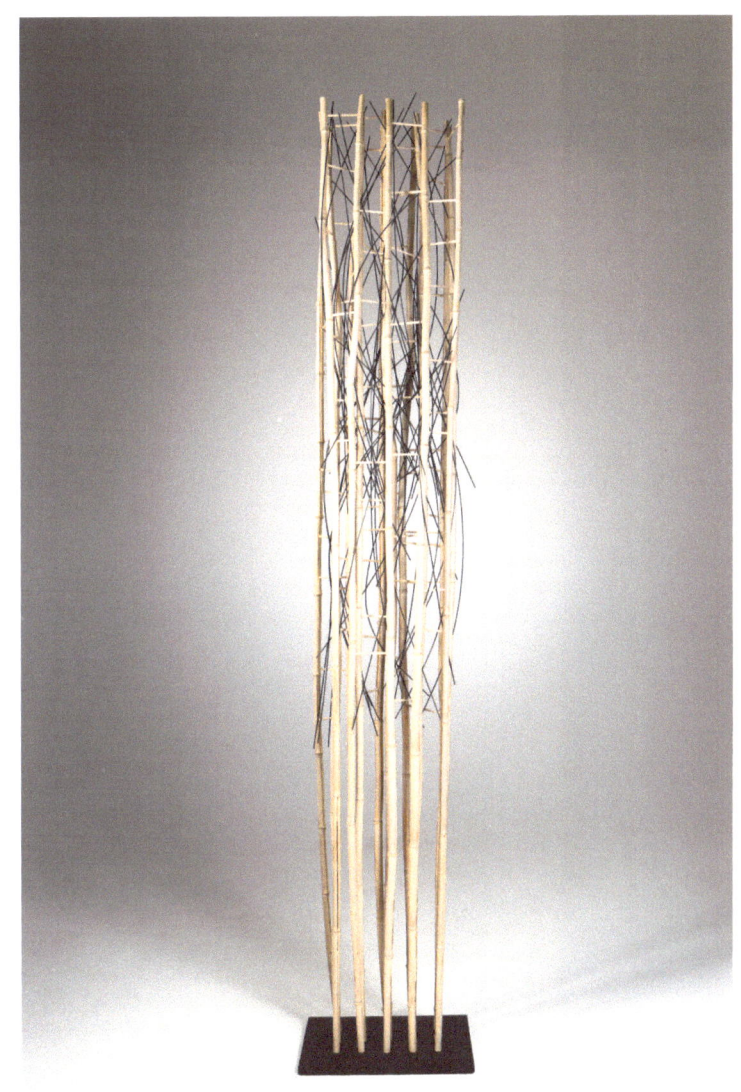

BAMBOO GROOVE

57.5H X 21.5W X 8D

Crafted of Cherry, Walnut, and PaperStone
2013

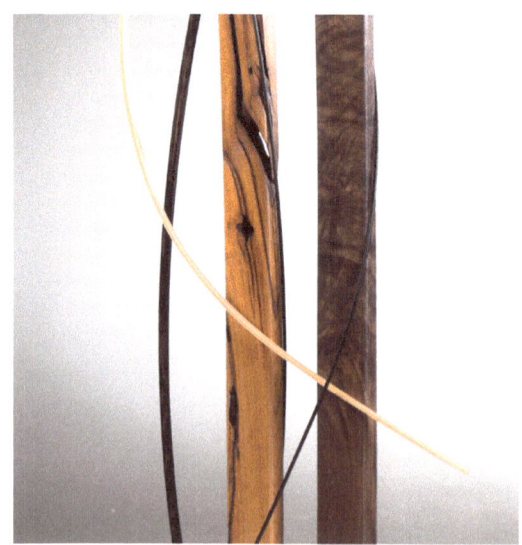

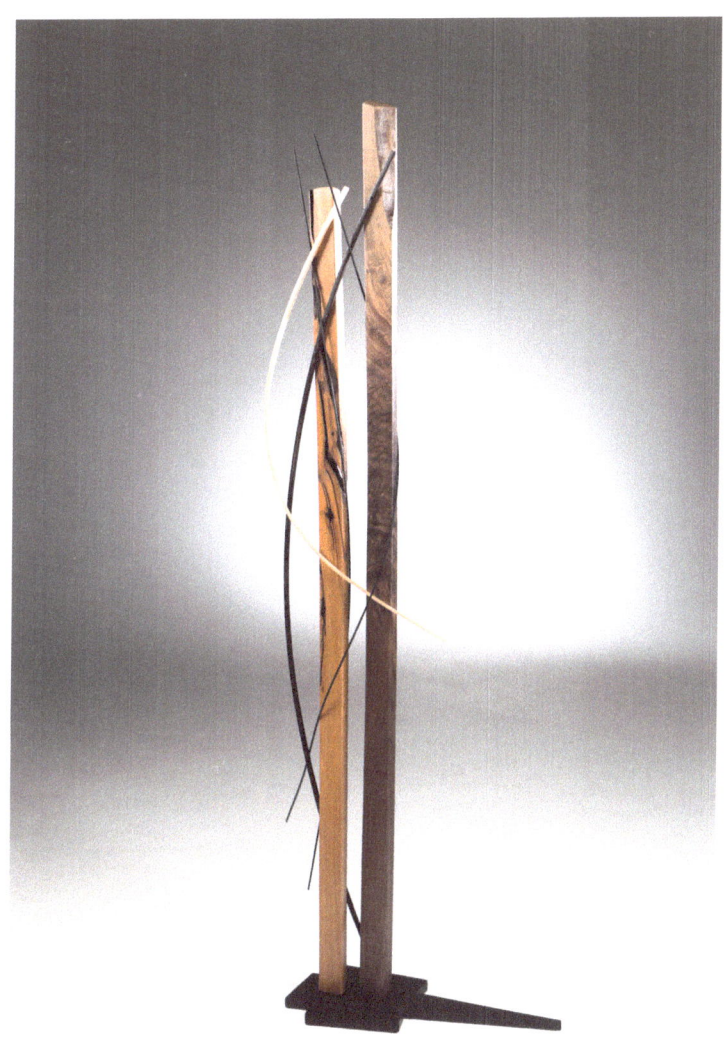

ANGLES AND ARCS

26.5H X 126W X 4.73D

Walnut and Various Woods
2014

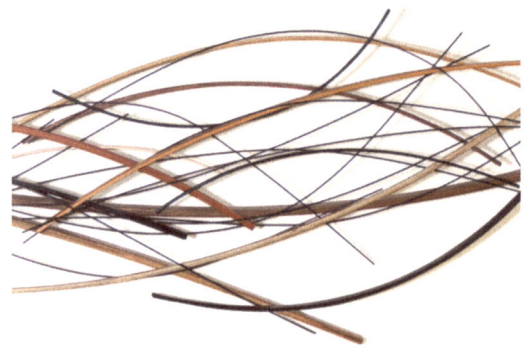

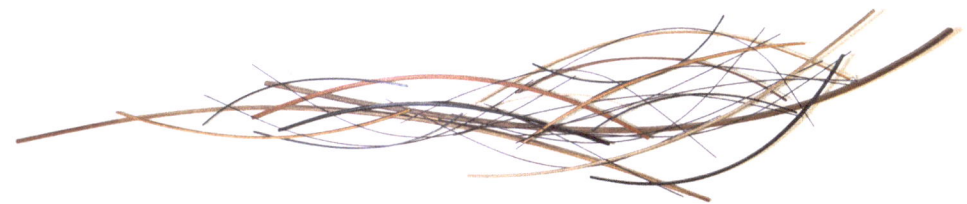

21H X 12W X 6D

Crafted of PaperStone and Maple
2012

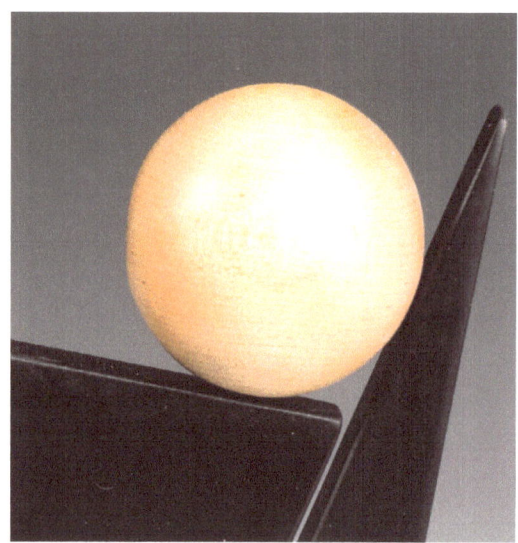

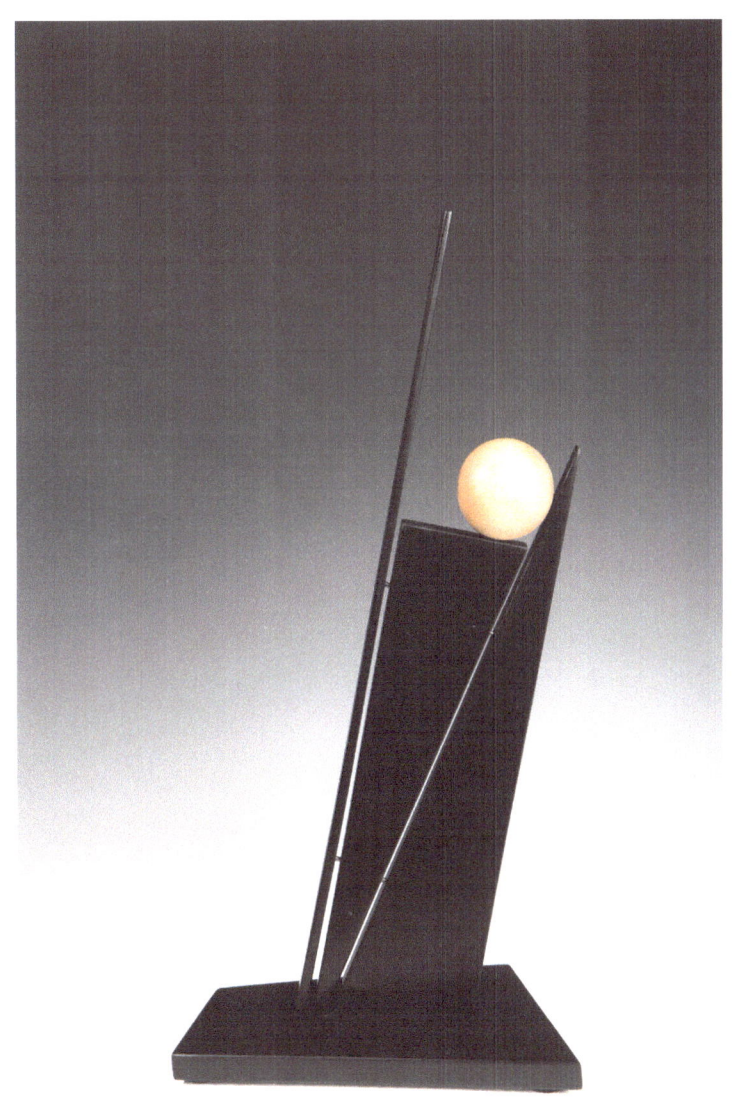

BALANCING ACT

33H X 31.5W X 16D

Crafted of Kirei, Oak, and Wenge
2007

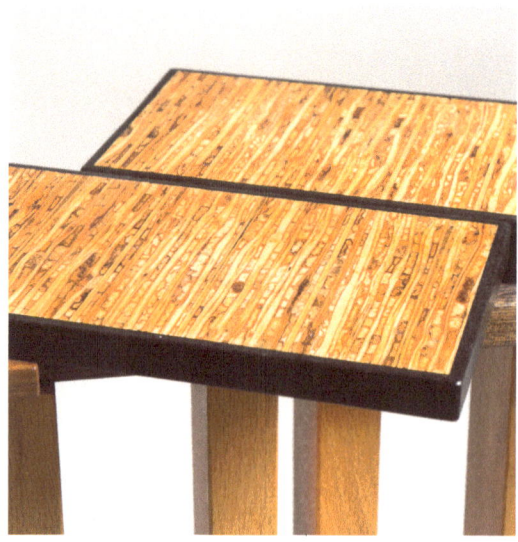

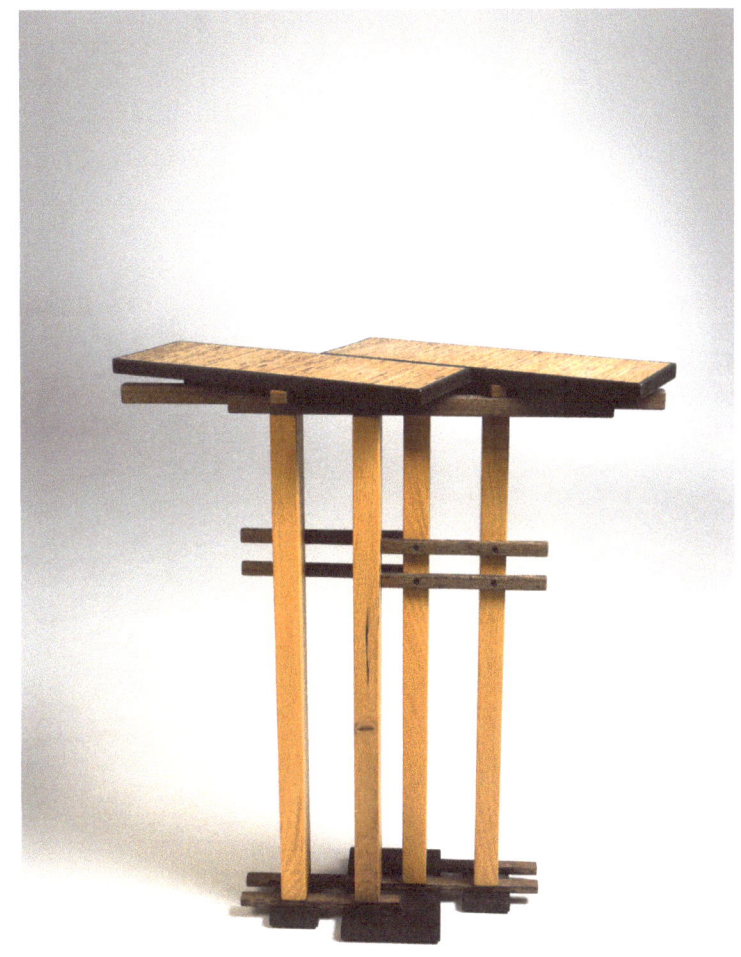

ZIG-ZAG TABLE

96H X 60W X 11D

Crafted of Painted Maple and PaperStone
2012

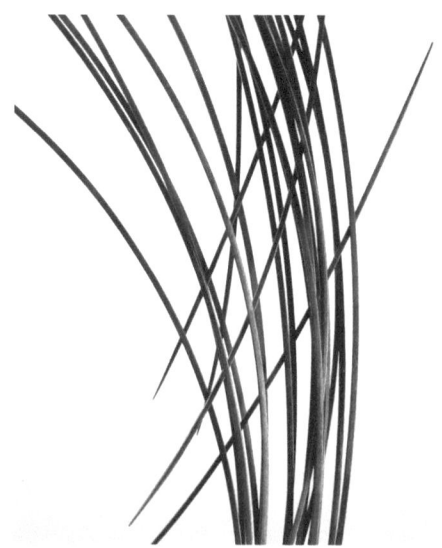

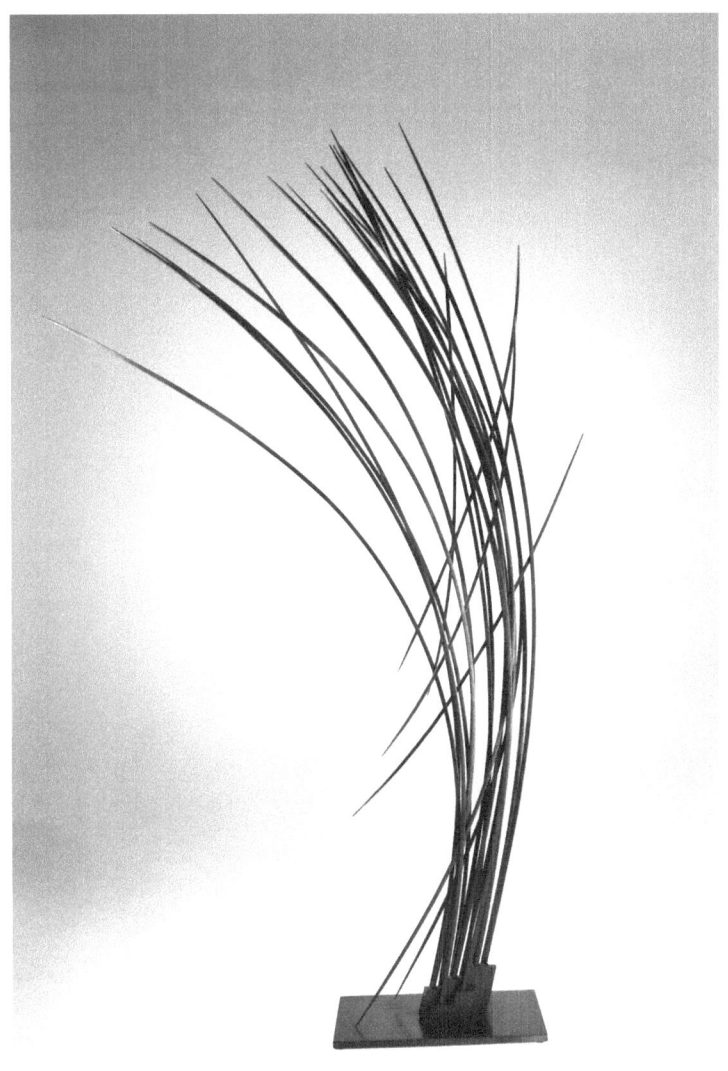

46H X 11W X 6D

Crafted of Walnut, Bubinga, and PaperStone
2010

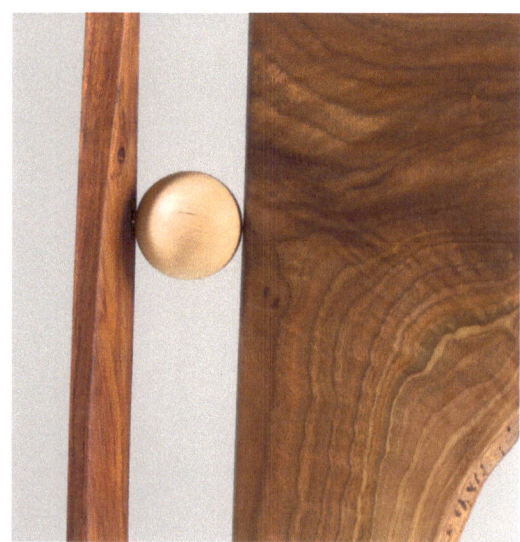

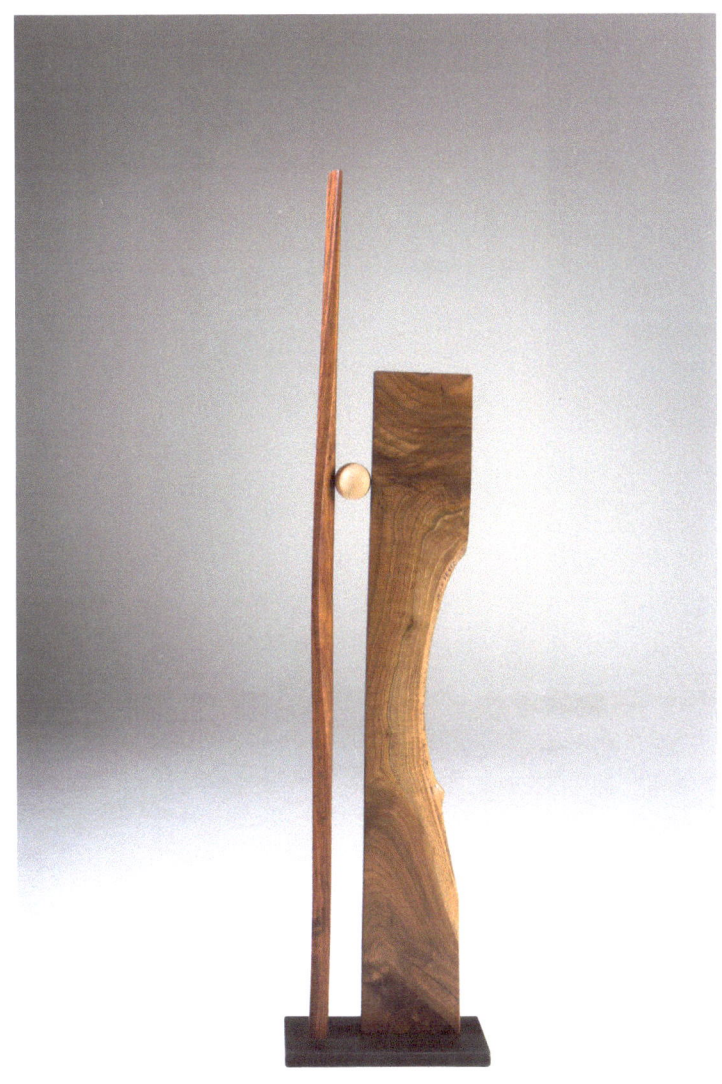

40H X 63W X 8D

Crafted of Maple, Walnut, and Various Woods
2007

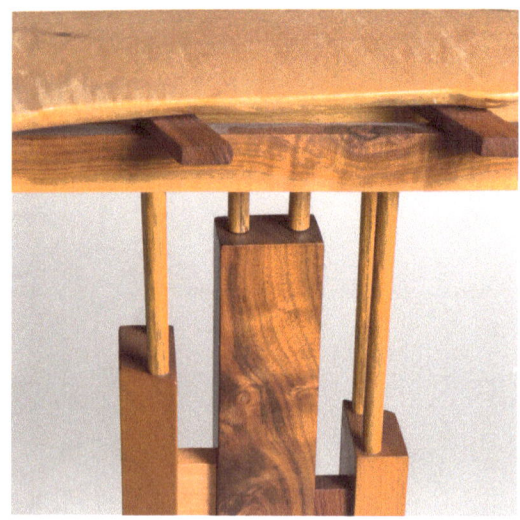

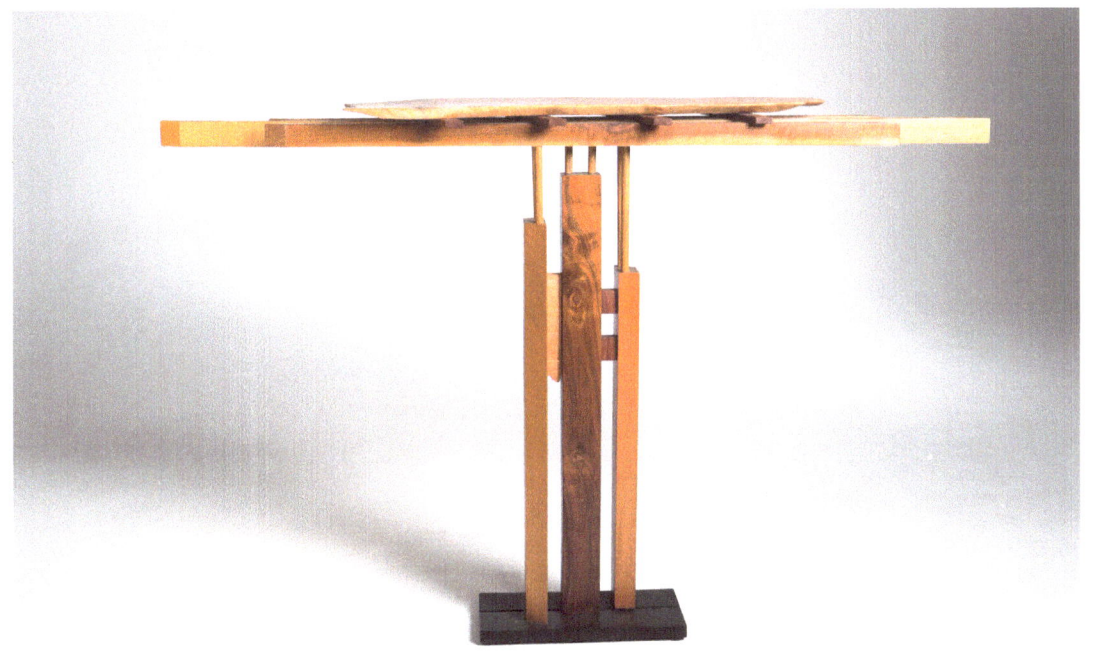

10H X 74W X 2D

Crafted of PaperStone and Walnut
2013

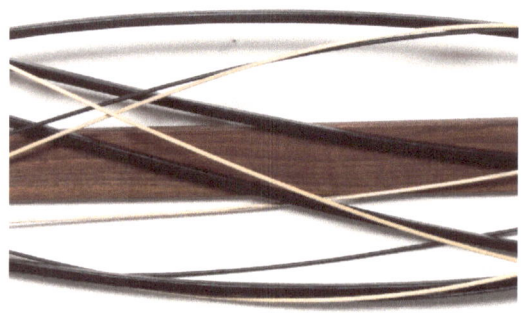

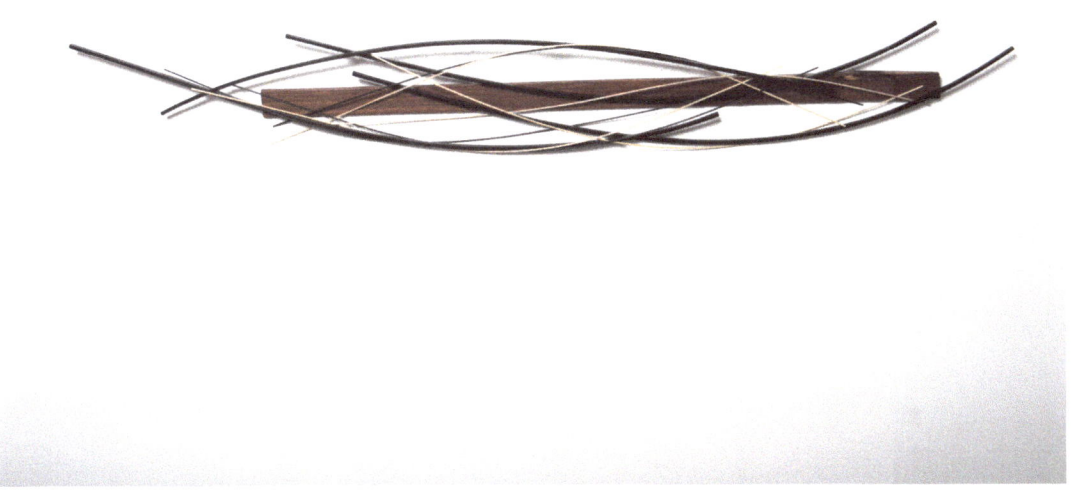

25.5H X 16.5W X 7.5D

Crafted of Environ Biocomposite and Aluminum
2007

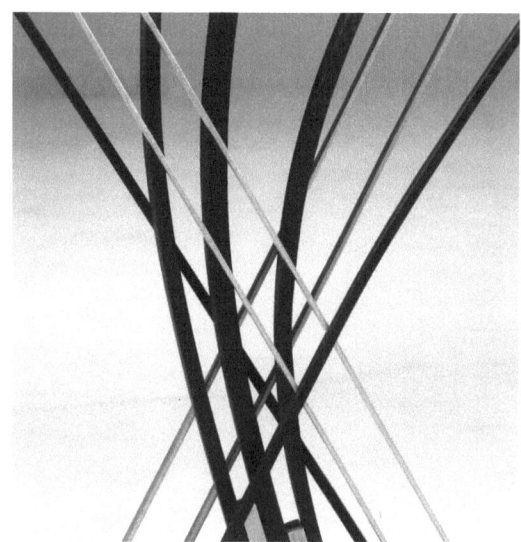

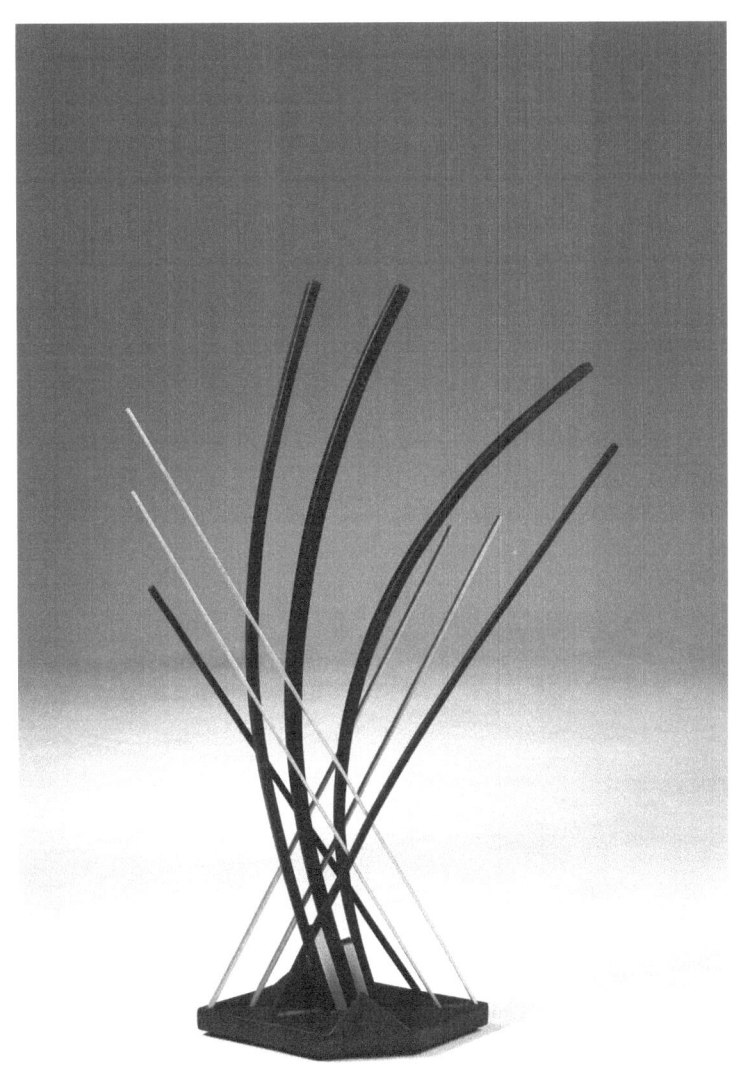

18H X 96W X 9.5D

Crafted of Cherry, Walnut, and Maple
2014

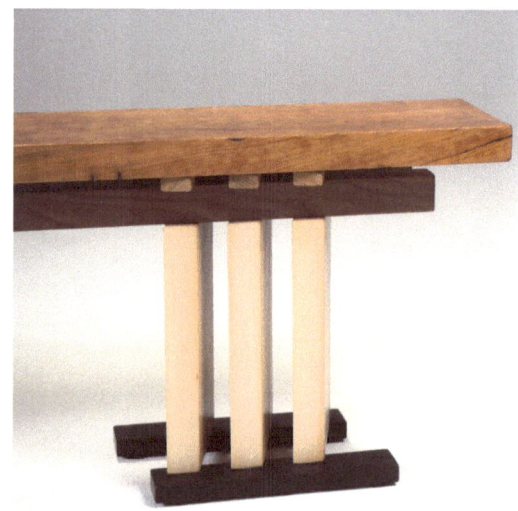

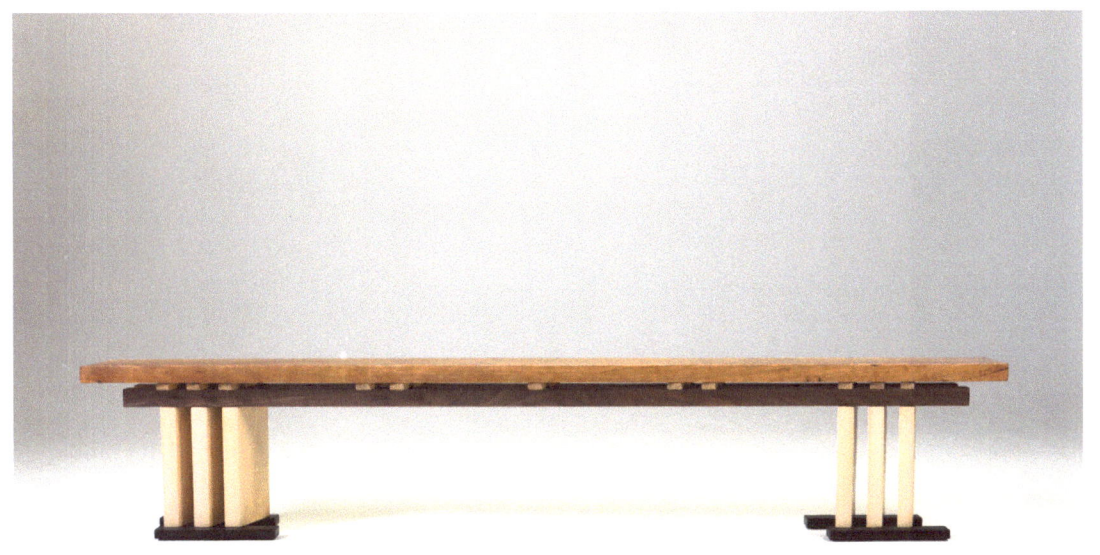

39H X 14W X 5D

Crafted of Mahogany, Walnut, and Limestone
2014

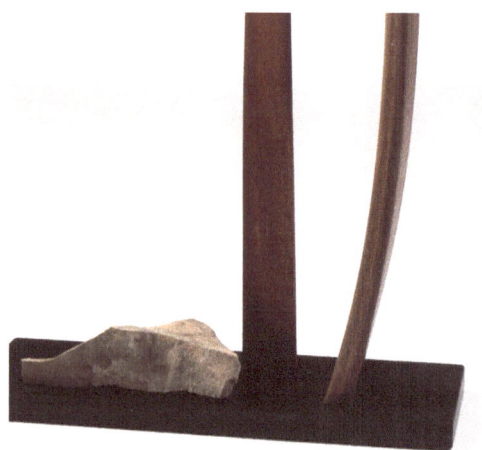

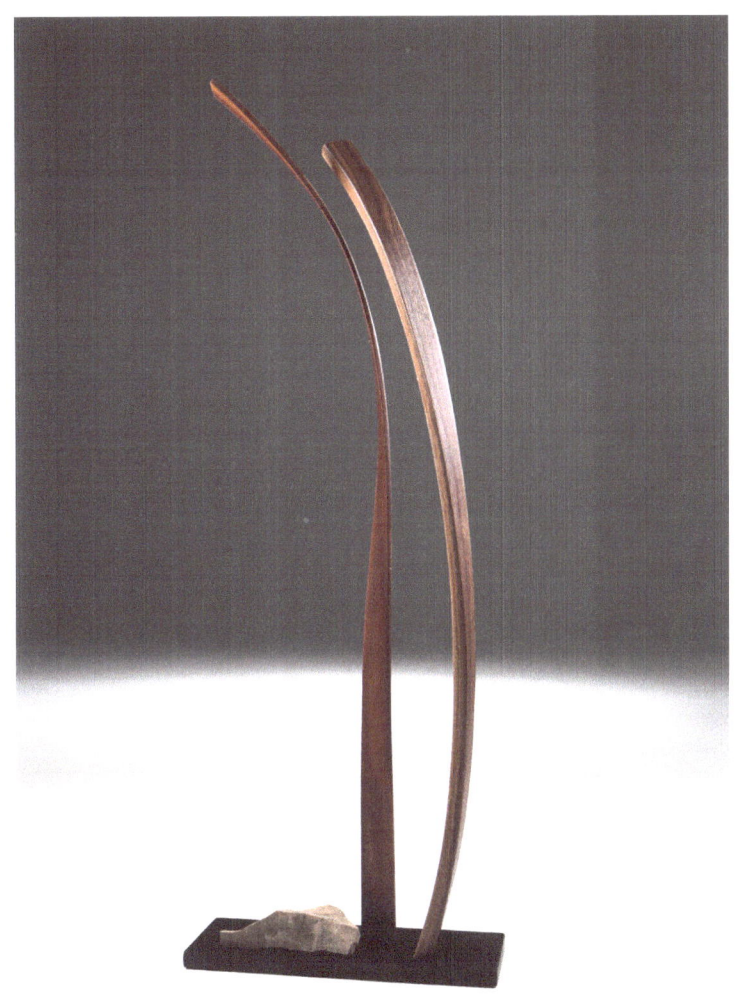

EARTH BELOW, SKY ABOVE

52H X 30W X 7D

Crafted of Painted Poplar and Cardinal Wood
2008

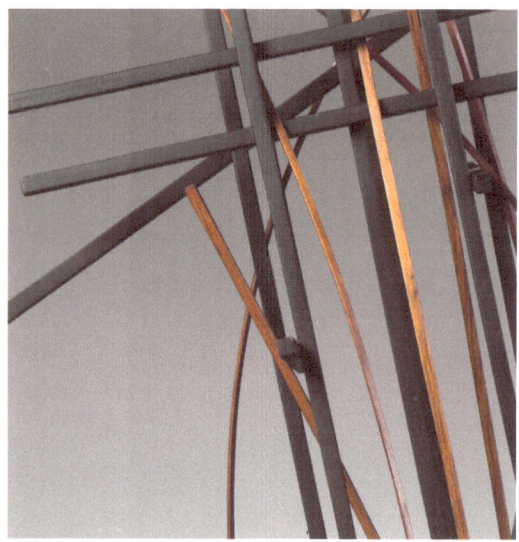

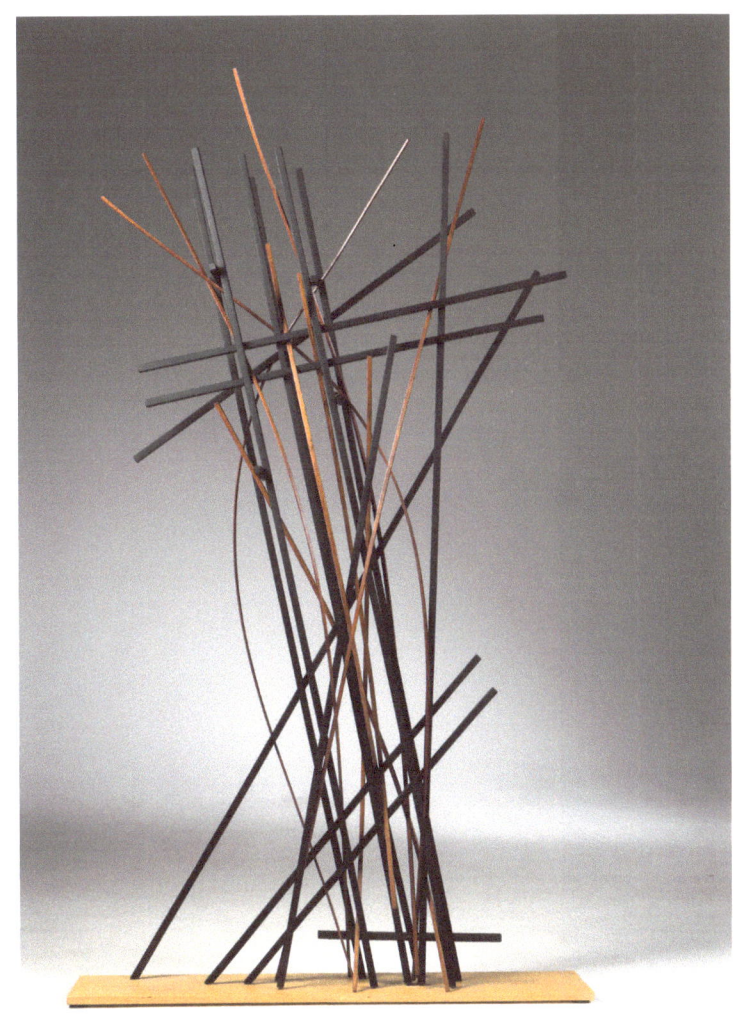

WALKING LATTICE

33H X 18W X 10D

Crafted of Environ Biocomposite
2007

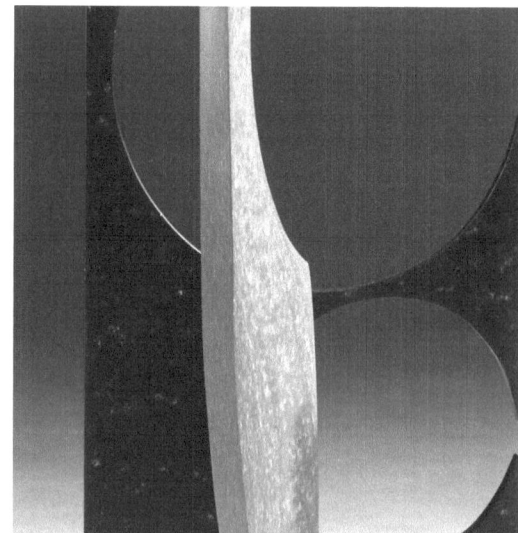

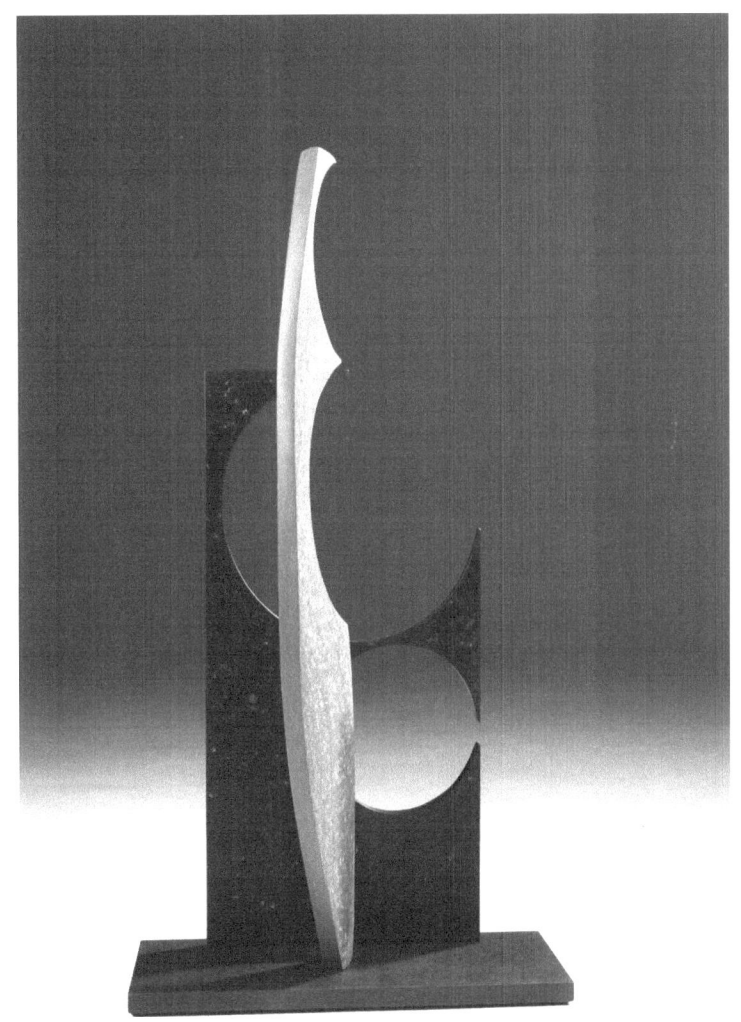

GEOMETRIC TANGO

78H X 54W X 42D

Crafted of Bamboo, Wenge, and PaperStone
2009

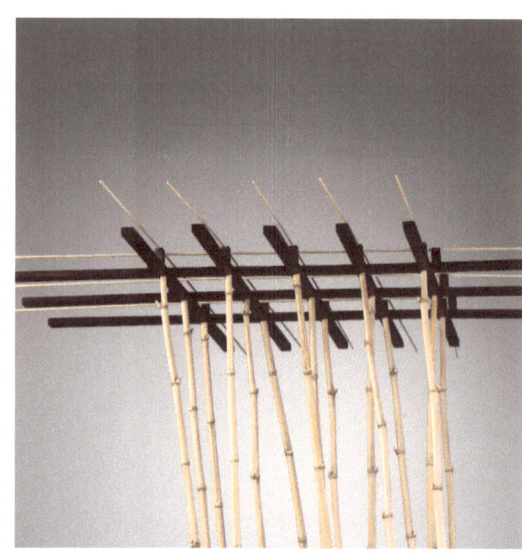

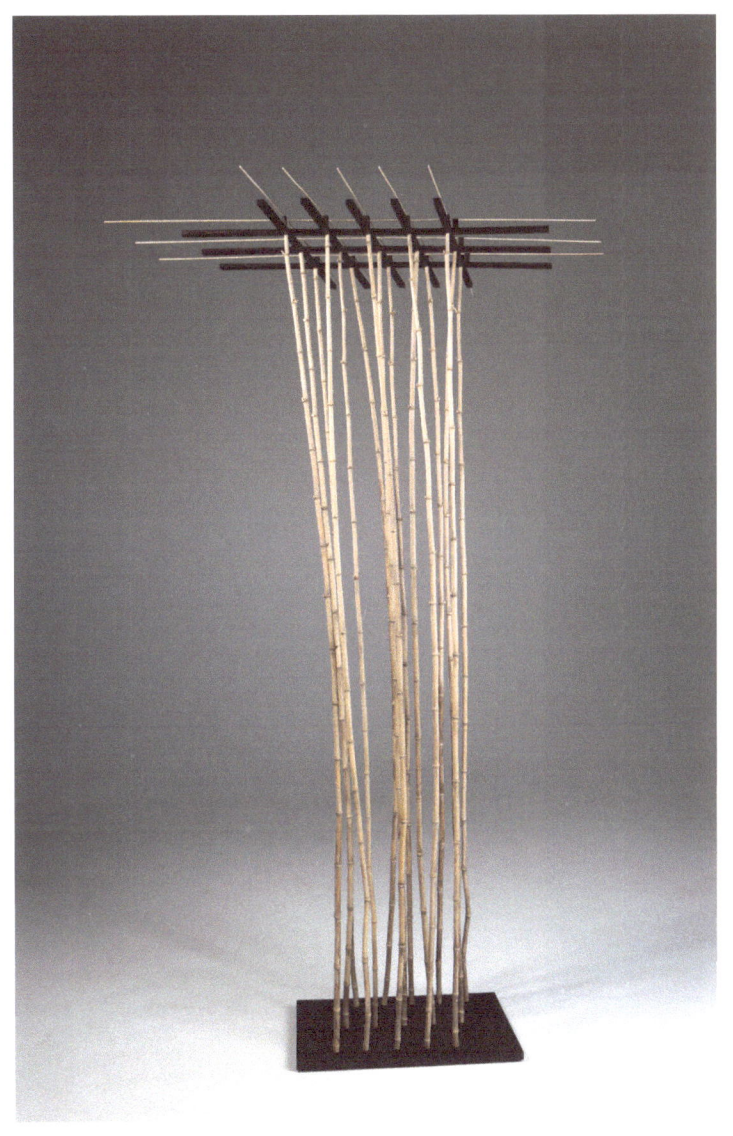

SKY GRID

96H x 76W x 19D

Crafted of Jatoba, Maple, White Oak, and Synskin
2010

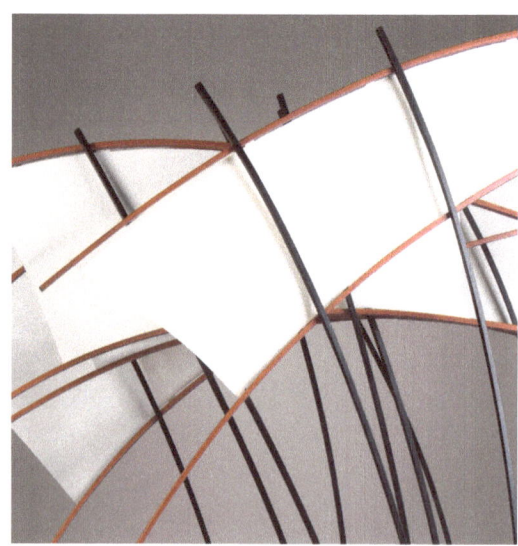

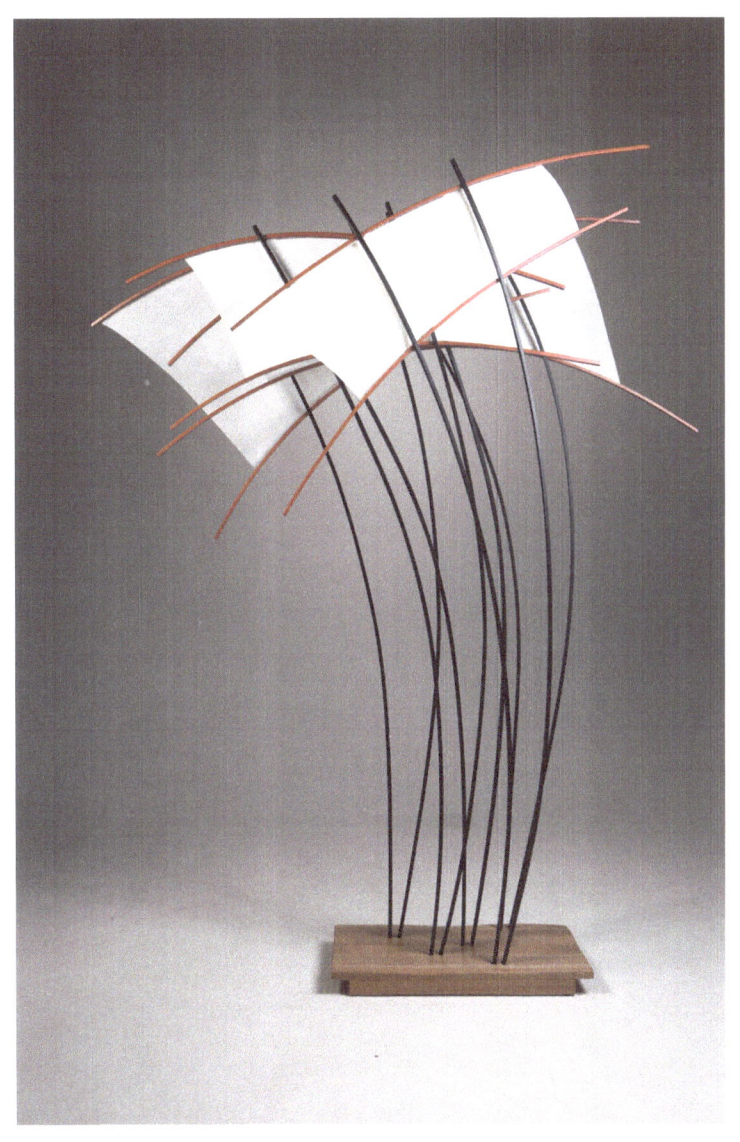

38.5H X 50W X 10D

Crafted of Rosewood, Cardinal Wood, Bubinga, and Wenge
2007

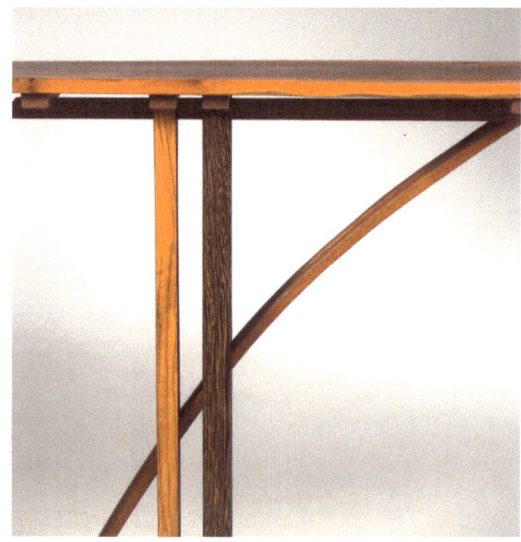

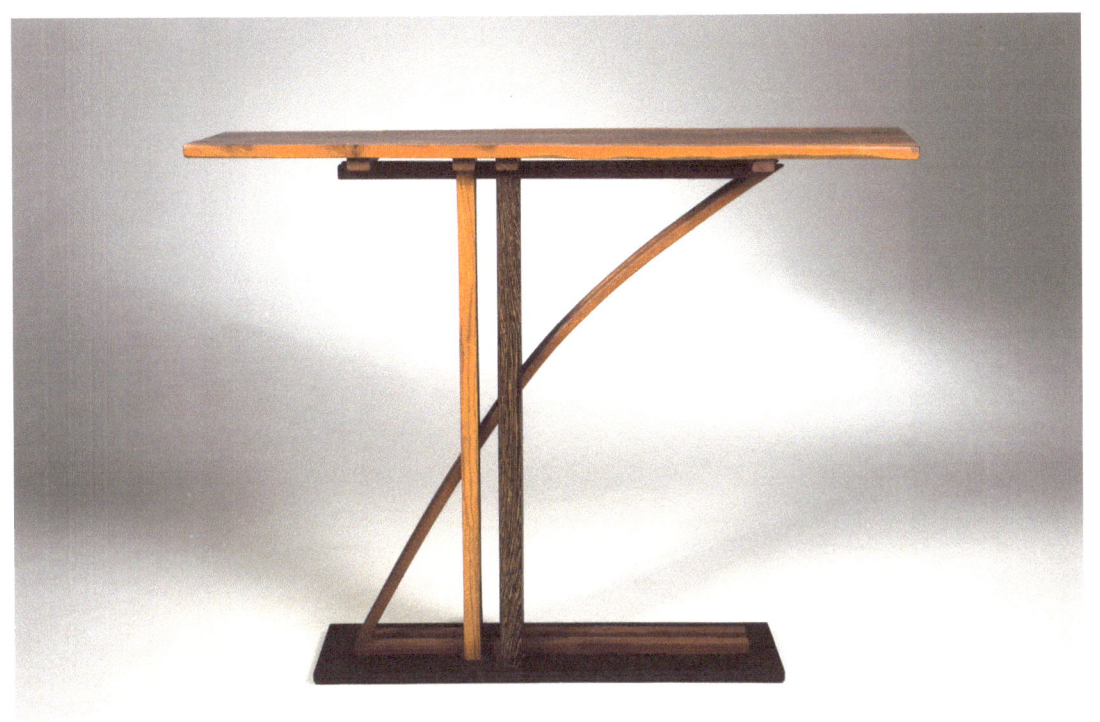

92H X 17W X 8D

Crafted from one Pine 2x4
2012

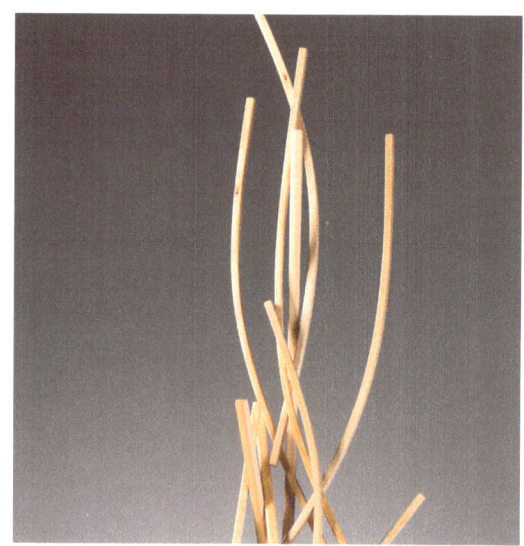

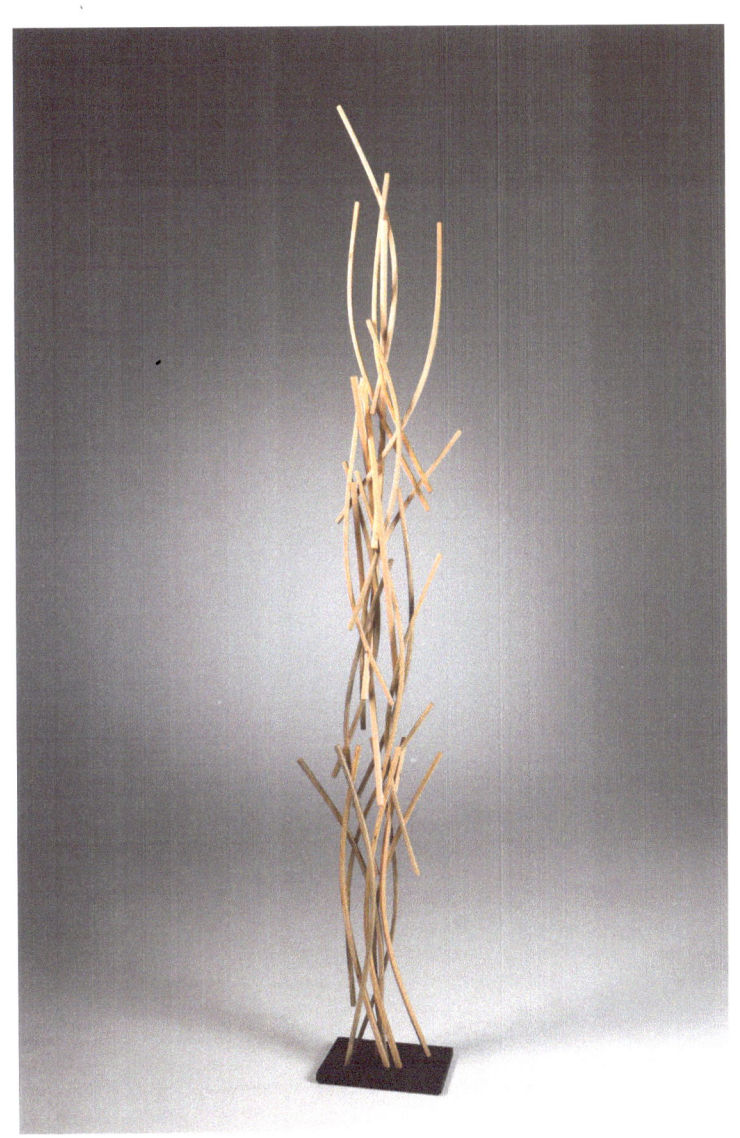

2 X 4 24

97H X 25W X 11D

Crafted of PaperStone and Various Woods
2014

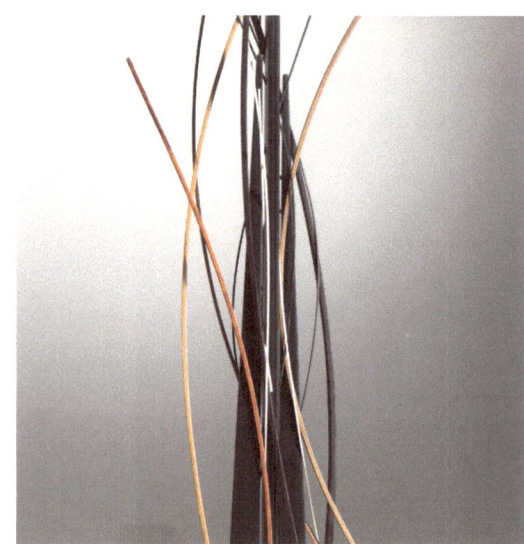

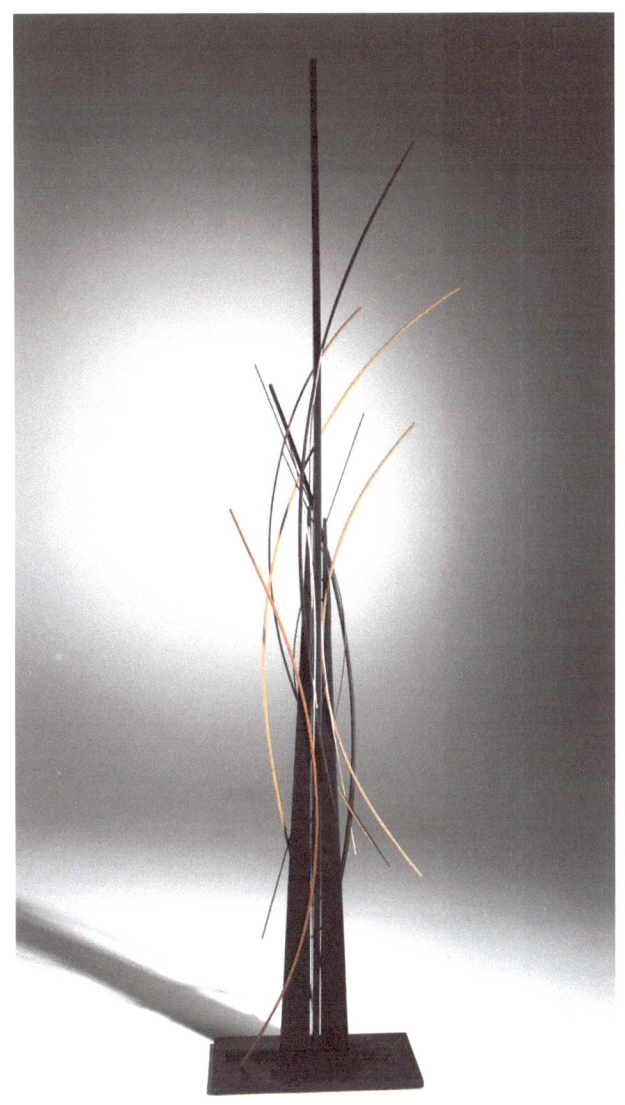

SILHOUETTE

37H X 8.5W X 5D

Crafted of Driftwood and Bamboo
2009

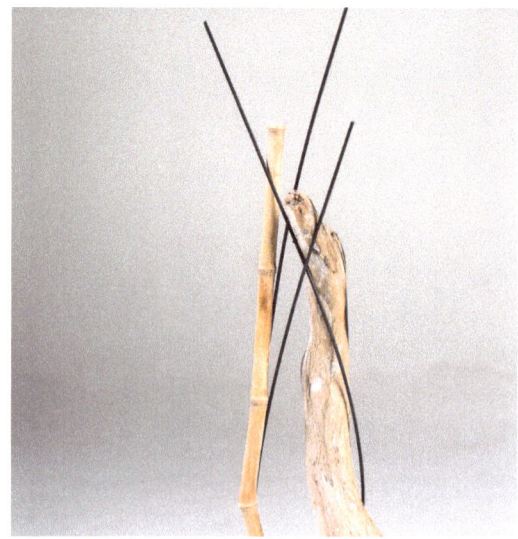

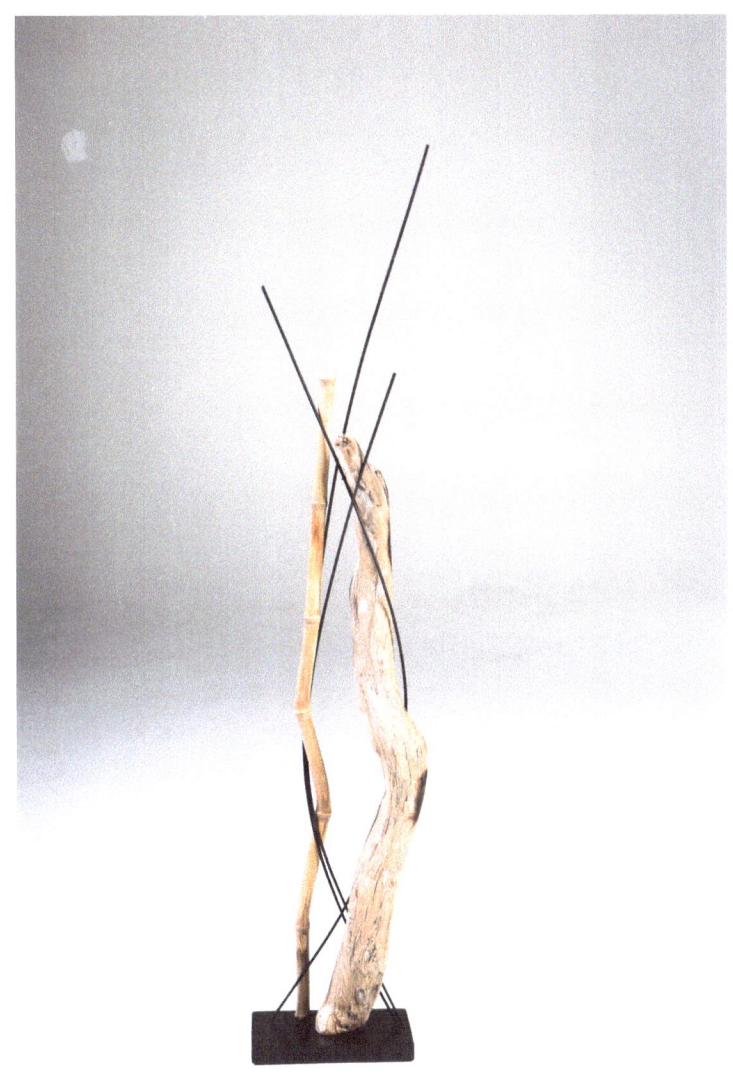

97H X 14W X 12D

Crafted of Cherry and Wenge
2009

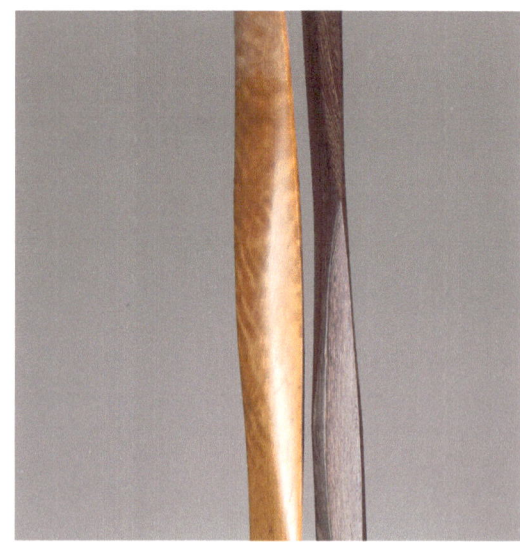

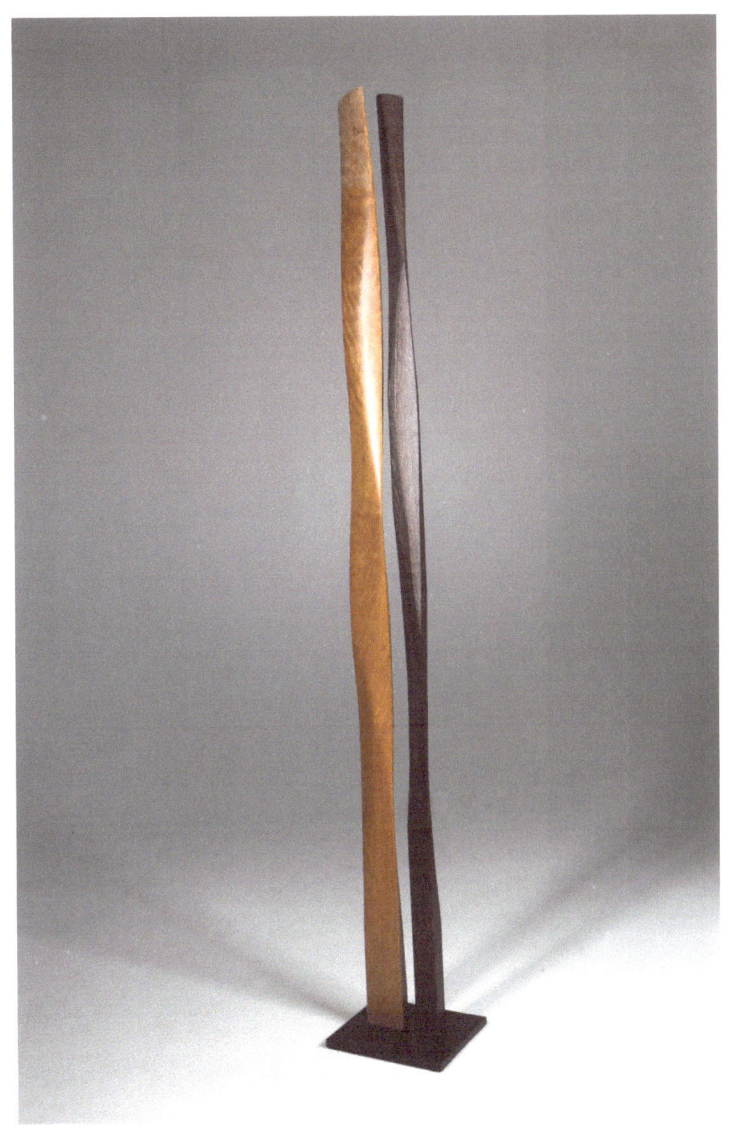

GRACIOUS DUO

13H X 91W X 2.5D

Crafted of Bamboo and Various Woods
2013

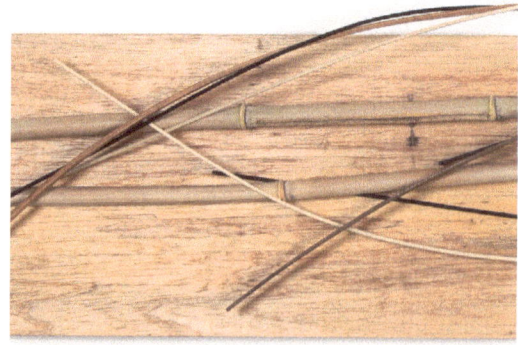

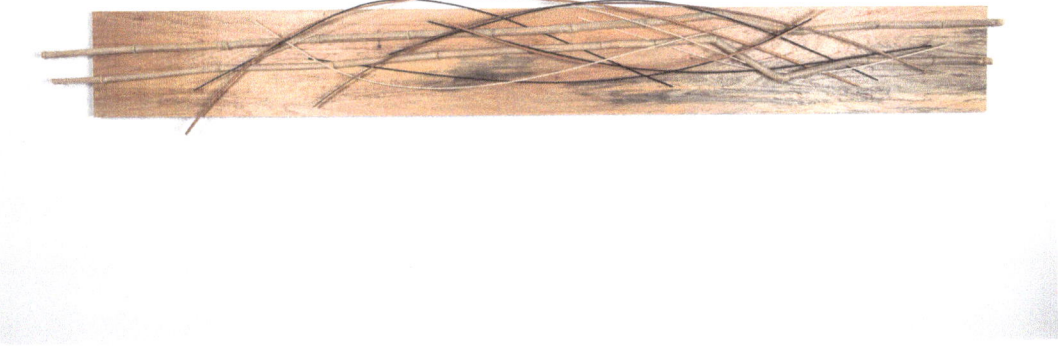

BAMBOO PANEL

39H X 51W X 9D

Crafted of Cherry, Walnut, and Bubinga
2013

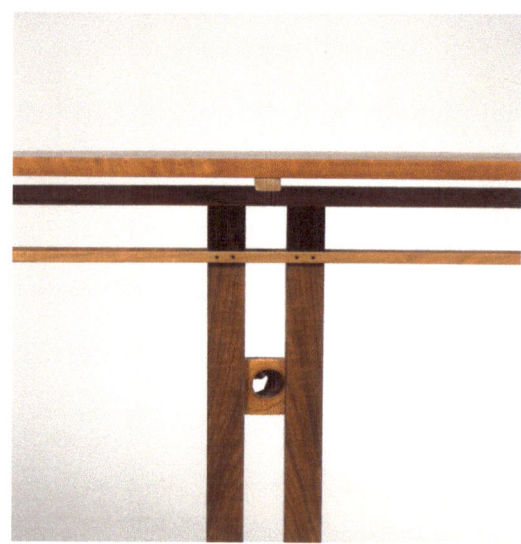

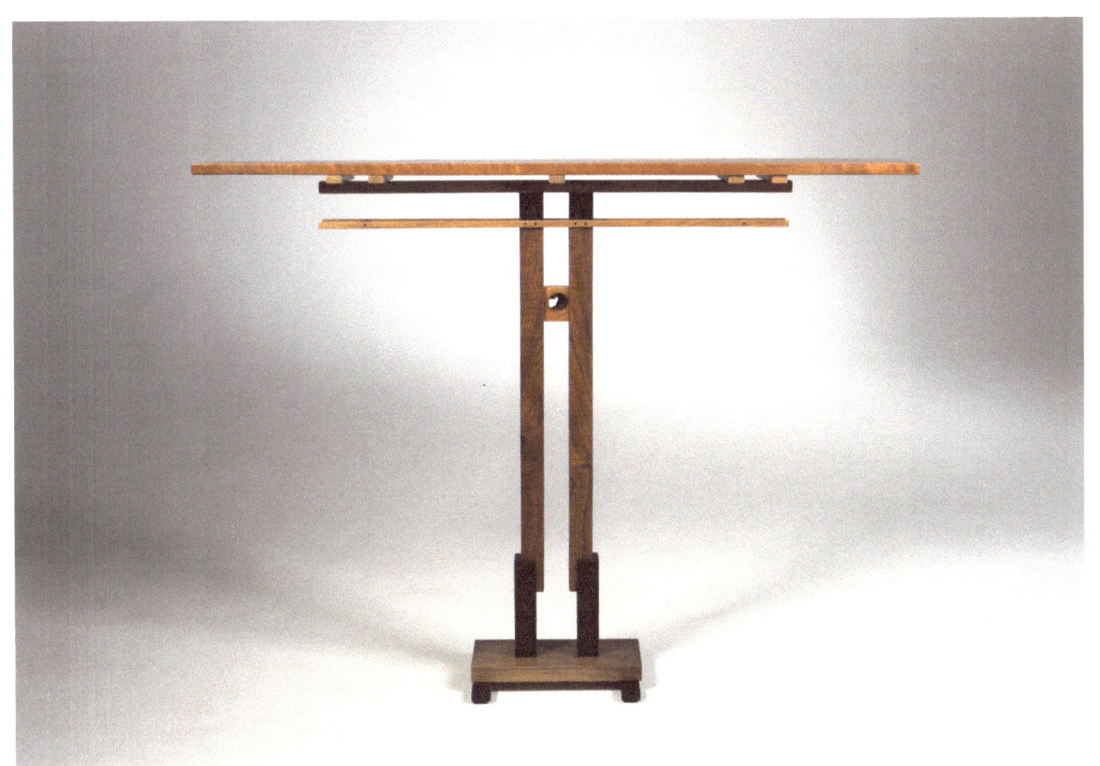

SAMURAI TABLE

73.5H X 24W X 18D

Crafted of PaperStone
2009

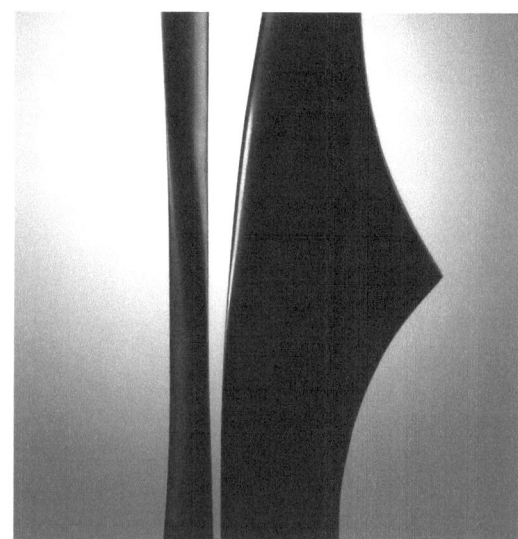

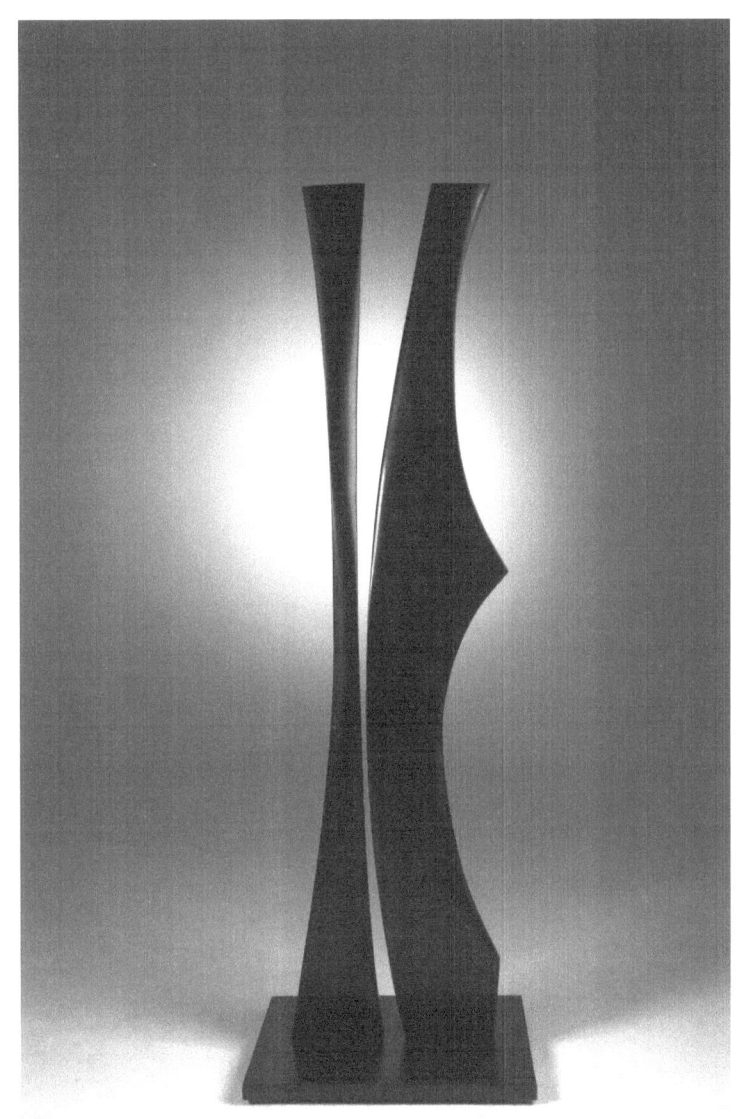

GEOMETRIC TANGO

84H X 15.5W X 14.5D

Crafted of Mahogany and Maple
2007

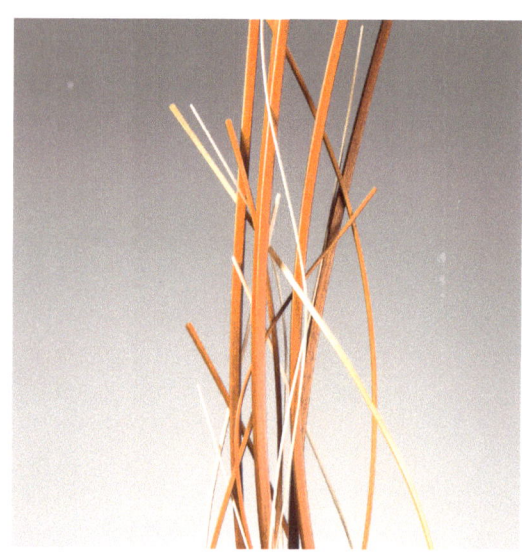

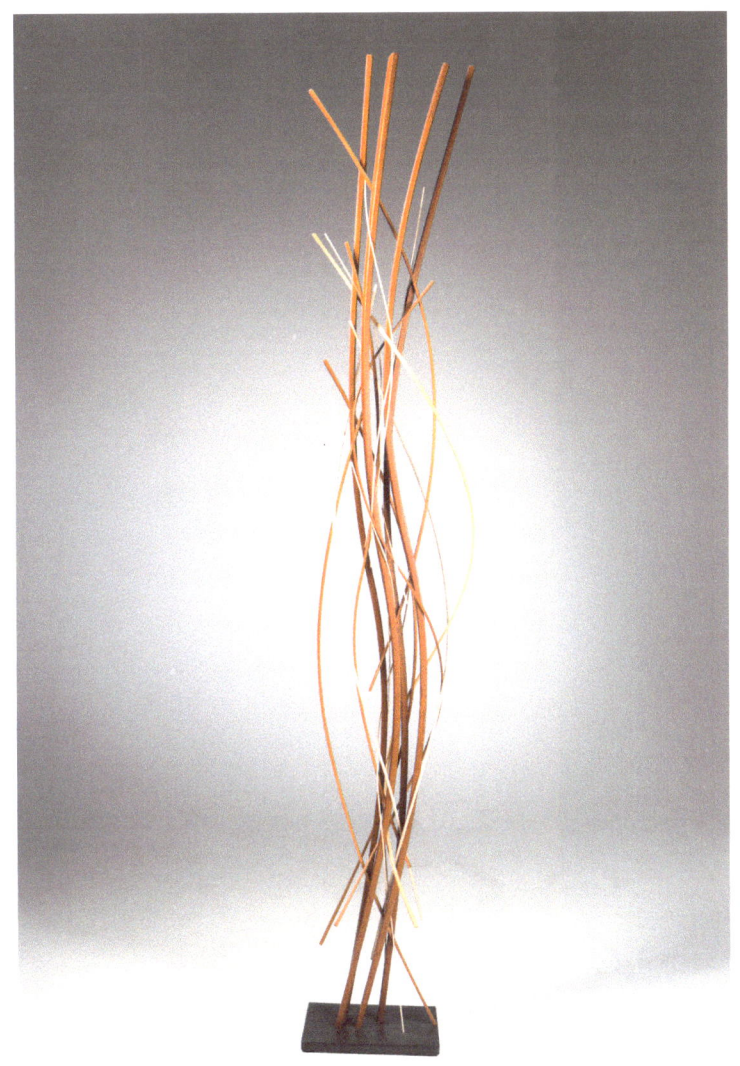

26H X 95.5W X 3D

Crafted of Plyboo, Walnut, and Various Woods
2014

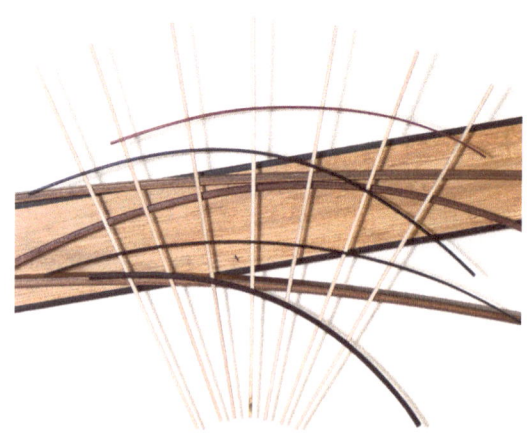

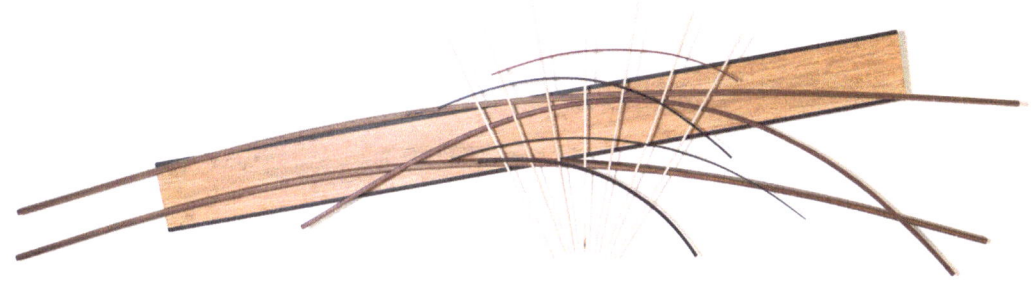

ANGLED WALL

47H X 6.5W X 4.5D

Crafted of Cherry and Walnut
2013

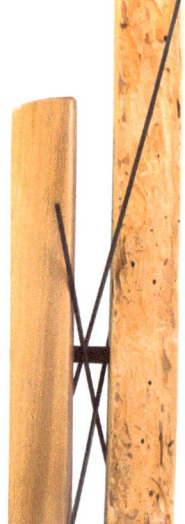

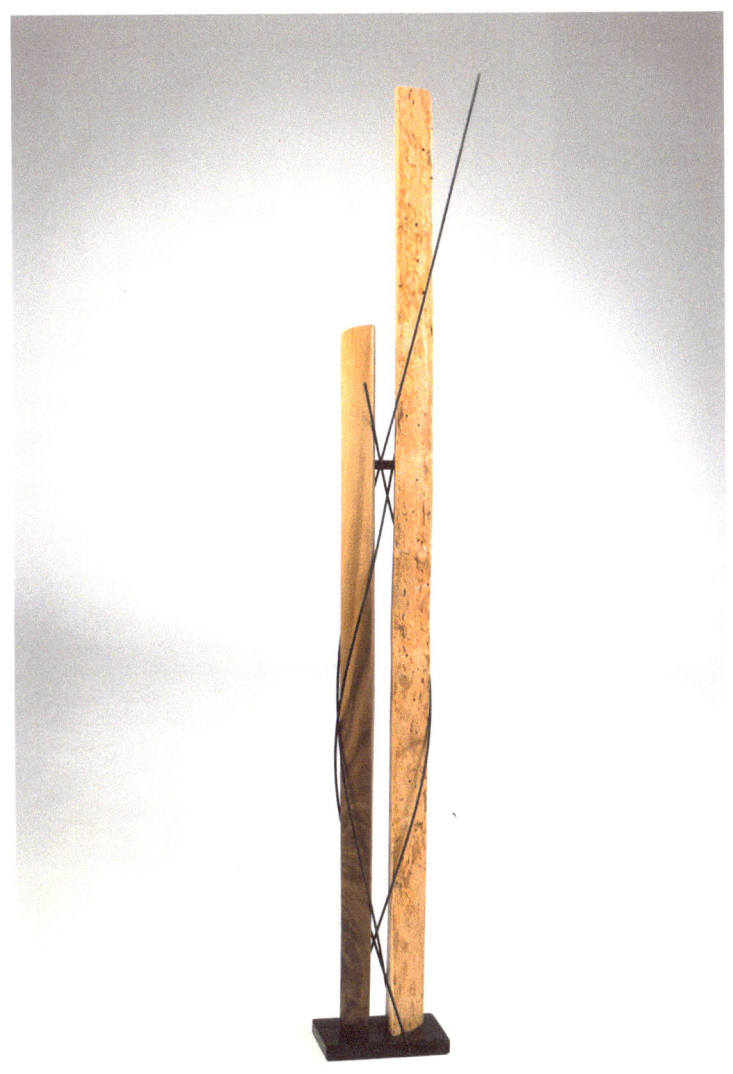

29H X 55W X 19.5D

Crafted of PaperStone
2012

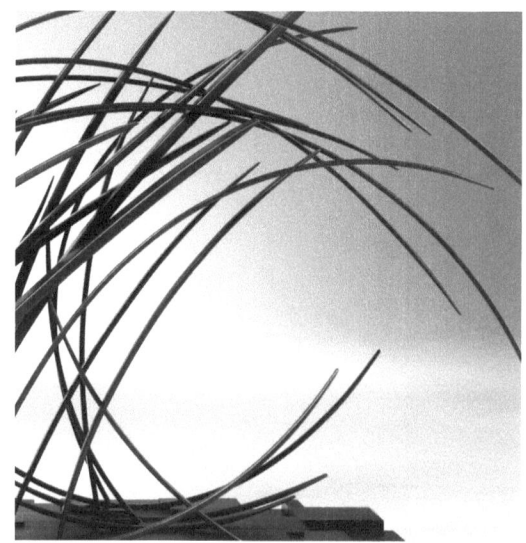

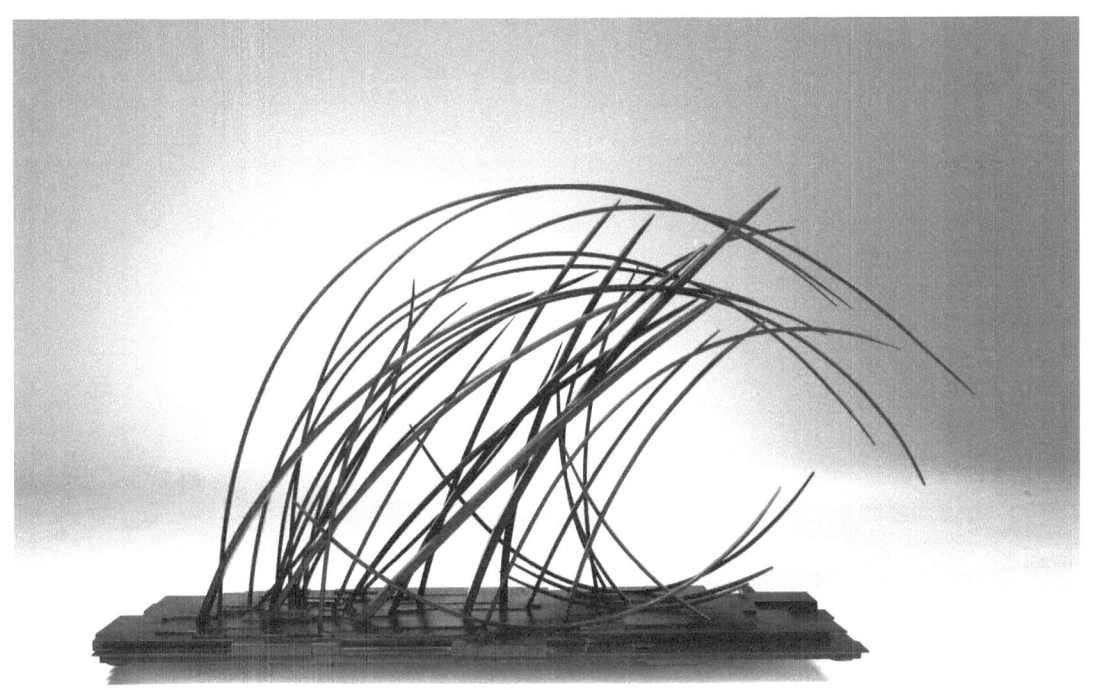

THE WAVE

30H X 108W X 7.5D

Crafted of Mahogany and Maple
2008

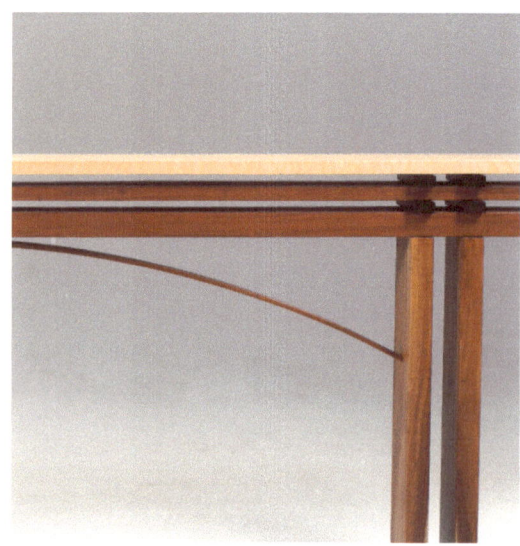

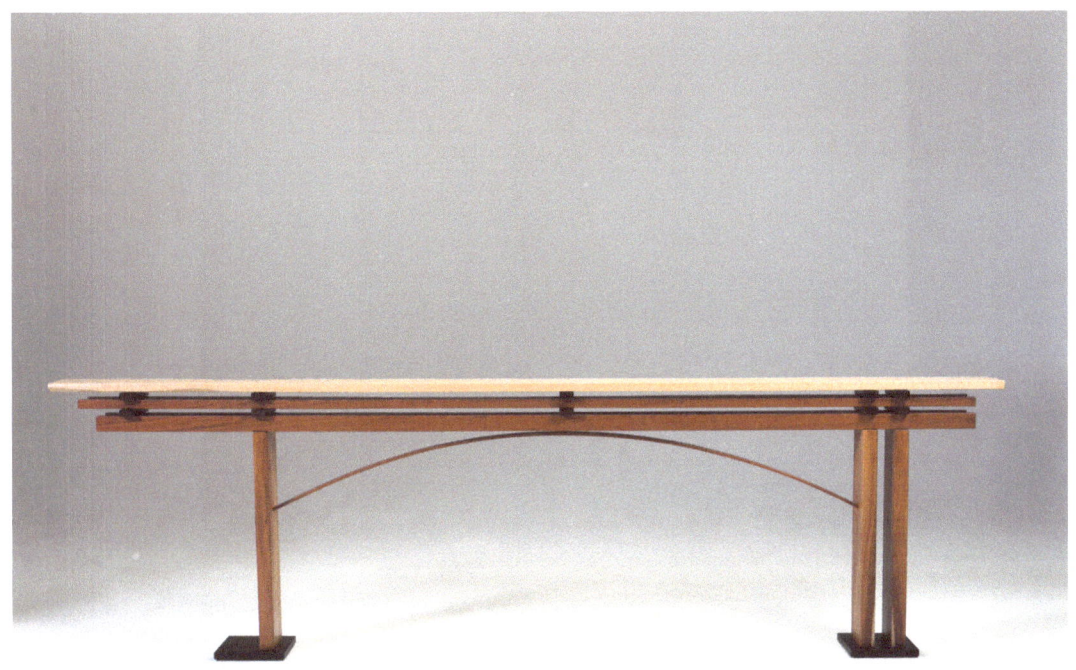

24H X 66W X 1.75D

Crafted of Walnut and Various Woods
2014

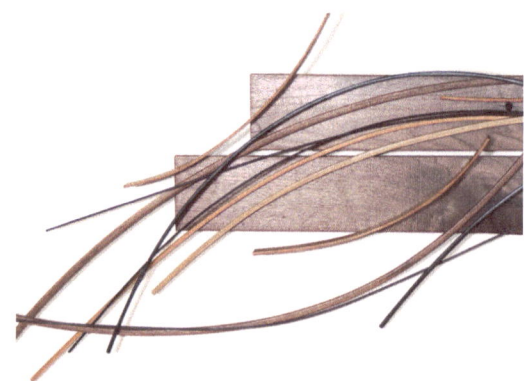

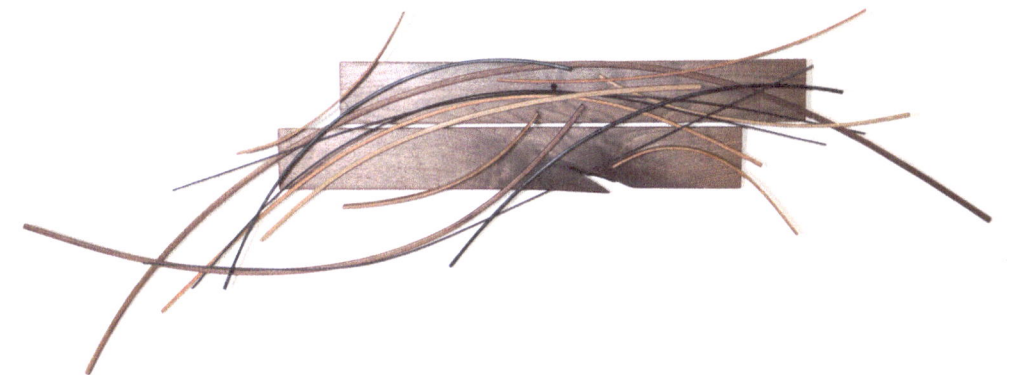

71.5H X 27W X 7D

Crafted of Various Woods
2008

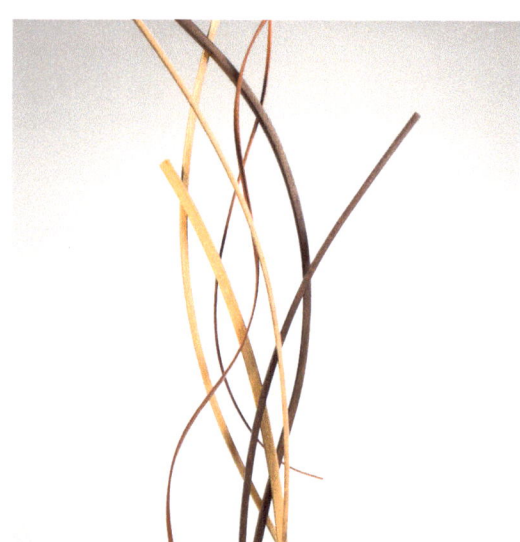

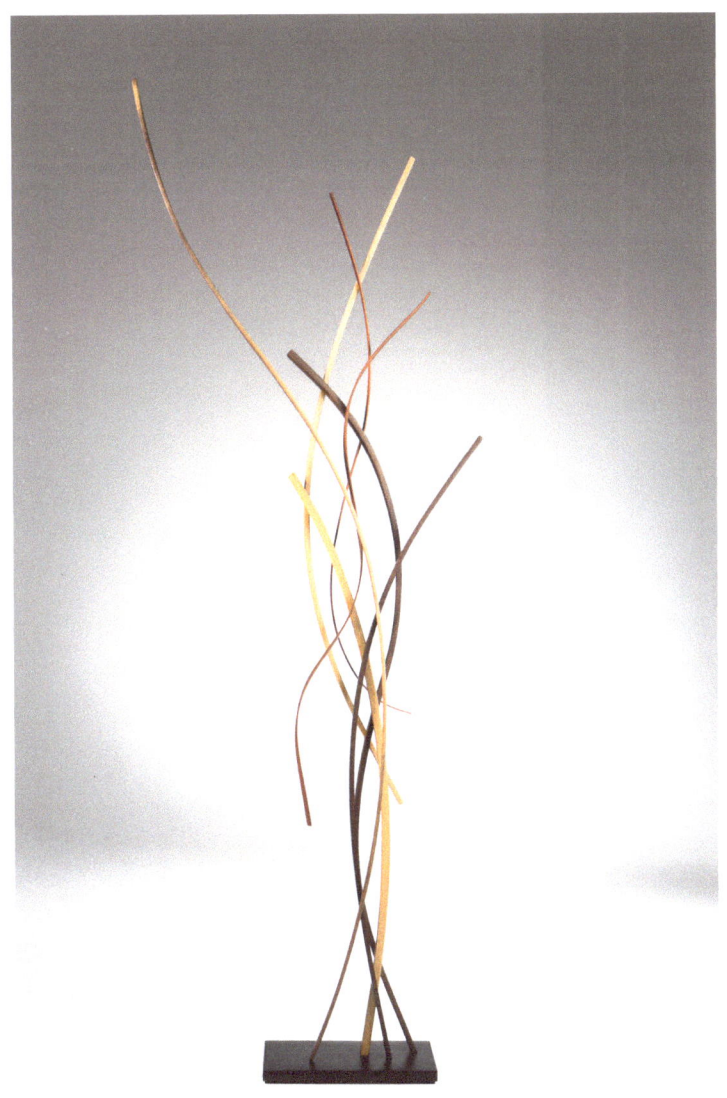

RHYTHM

35.5H X 8W X 4D

Crafted of Various Woods
2009

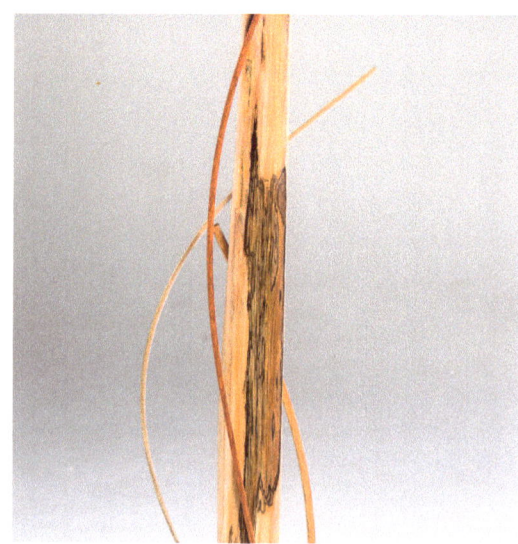

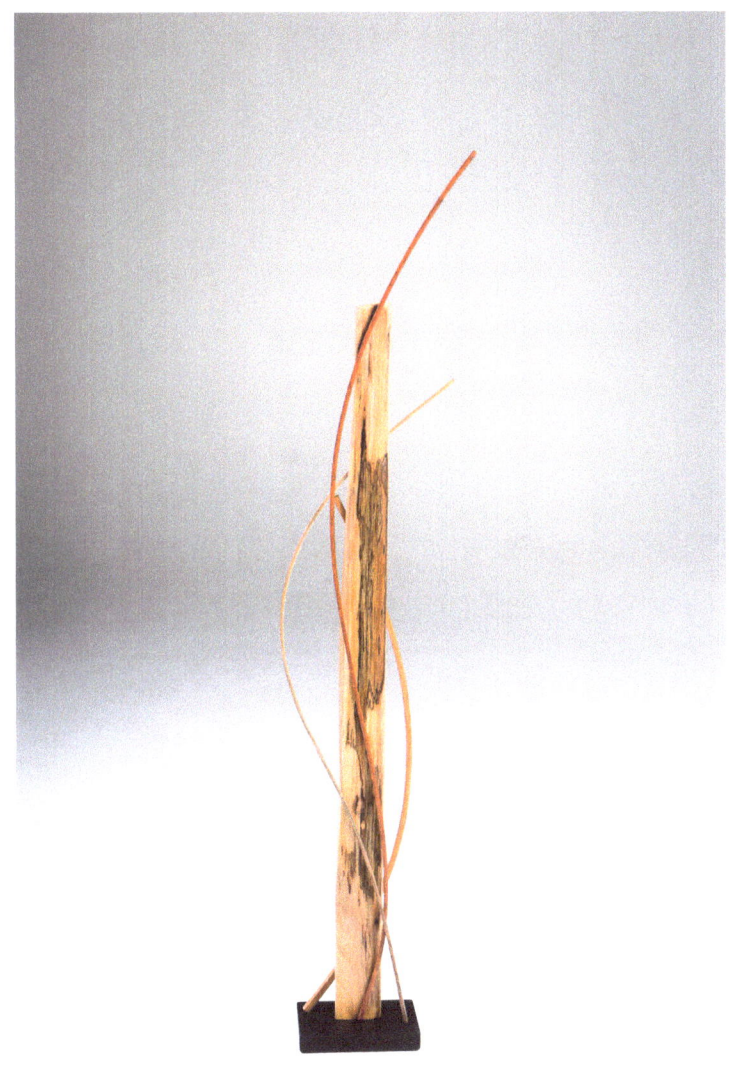

41H X 43.5W X 9D

Crafted of Zebra Wood, Environ, and Various Woods
2007

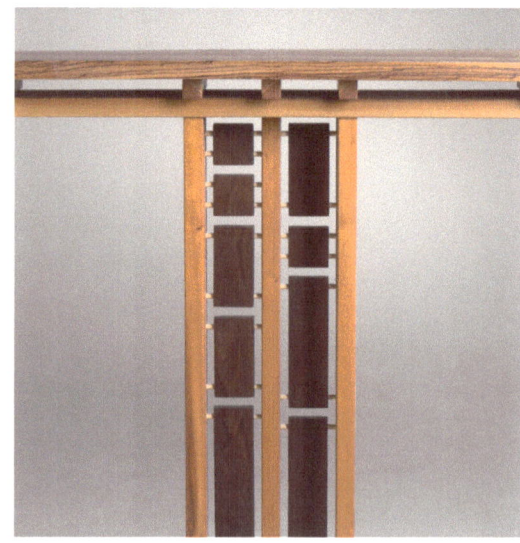

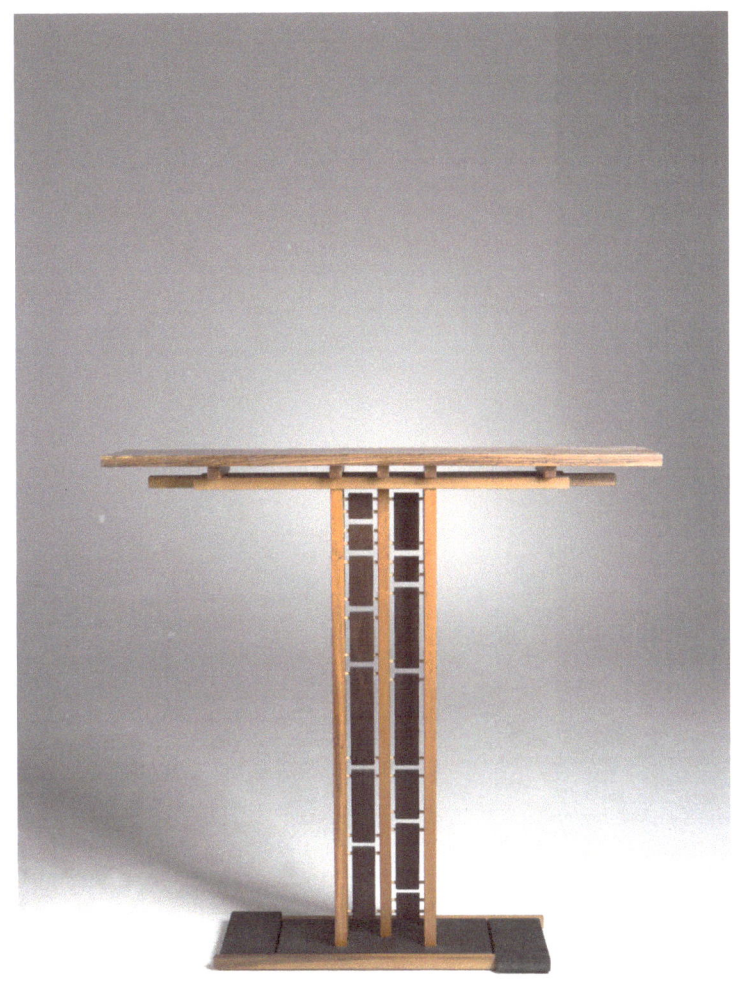

GRID TABLE

37H X 12W X 10D

Crafted of PaperStone and Maple
2012

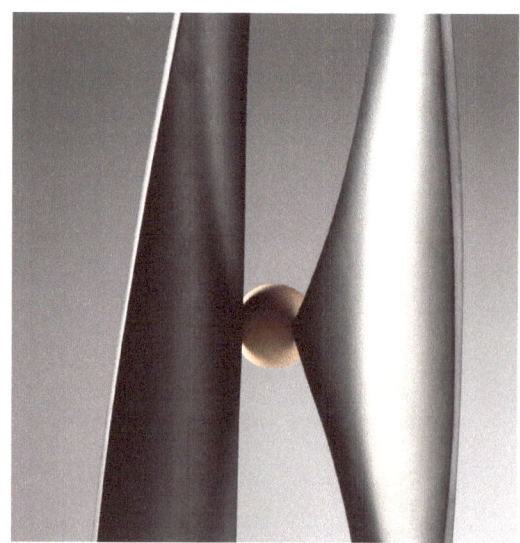

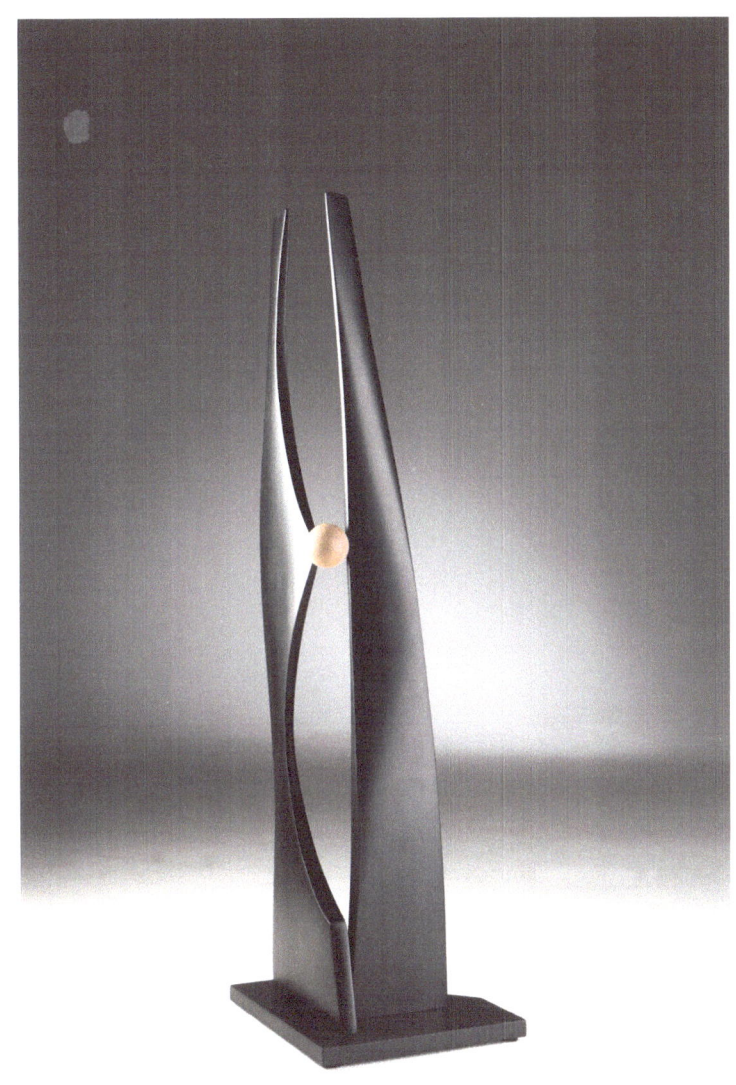

GEOMETRIC TANGO

21.5H X 82W X 5D

Crafted of PaperStone and Mahogany
2012

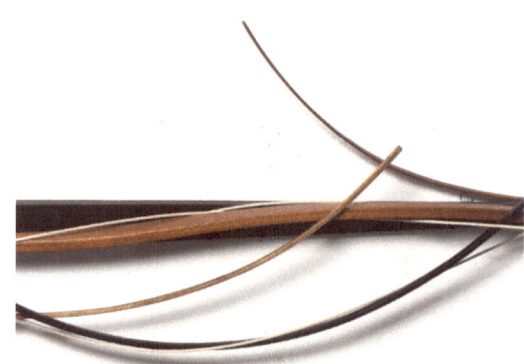

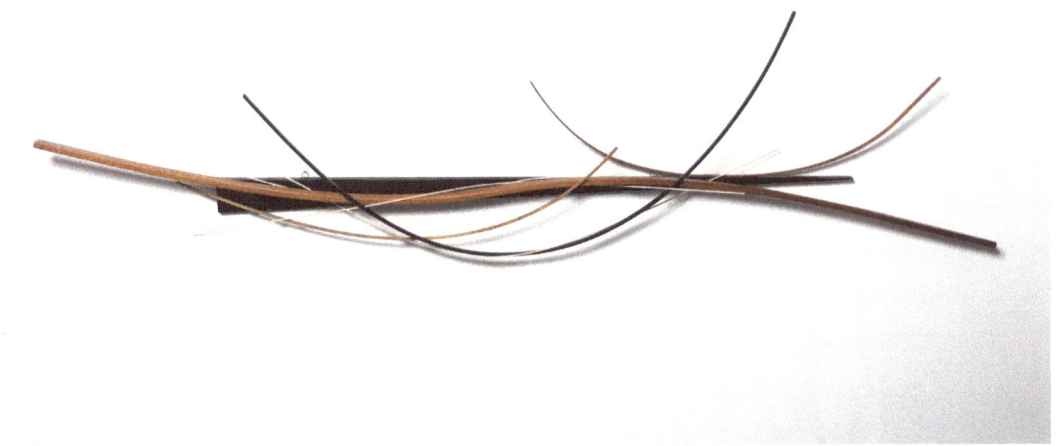

WEDGED ARC

96H X 32W X 10D

Crafted of Painted Maple and PaperStone
2012

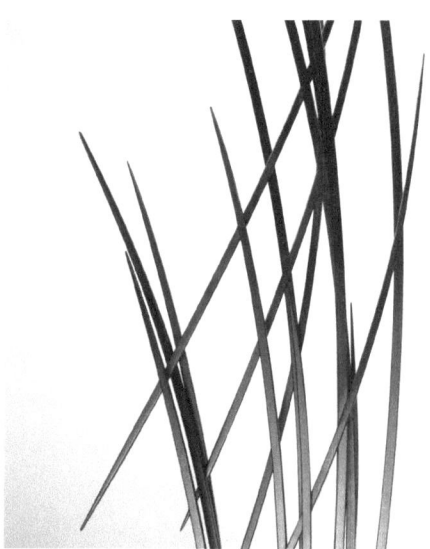

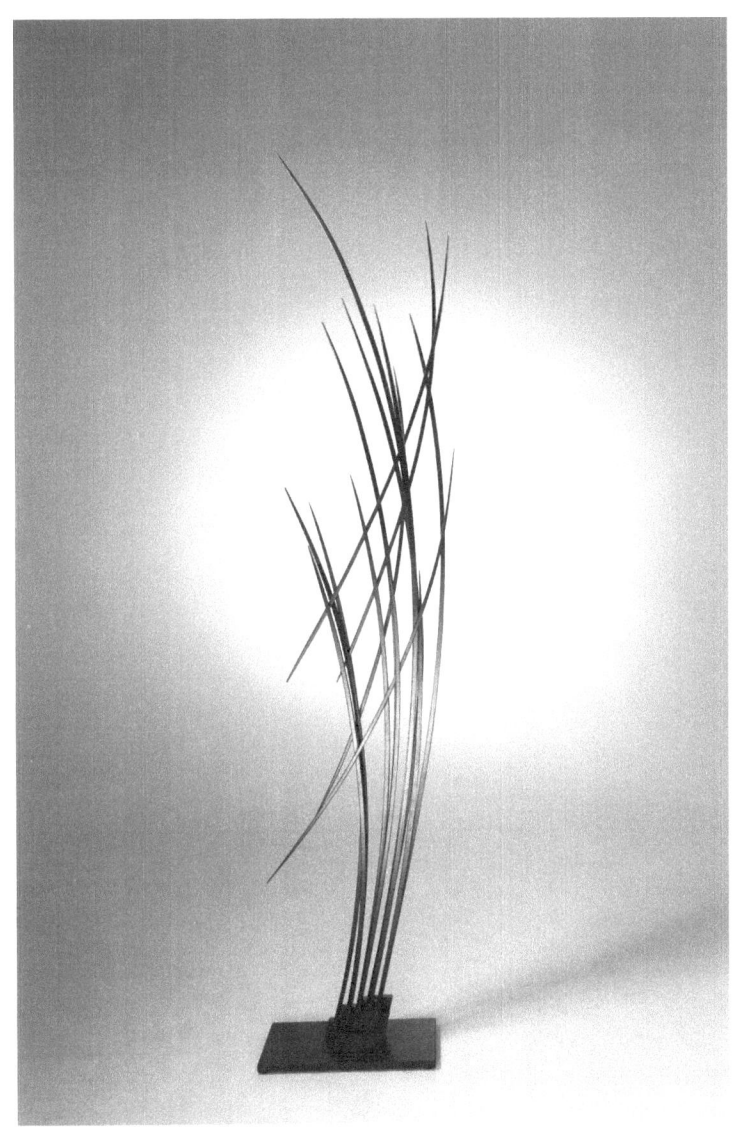

SMALL VERTICAL ARC

18H X 73W X 10D

Crafted of Indonesian Rosewood, Aluminum, Bubinga, and Wenge
2013

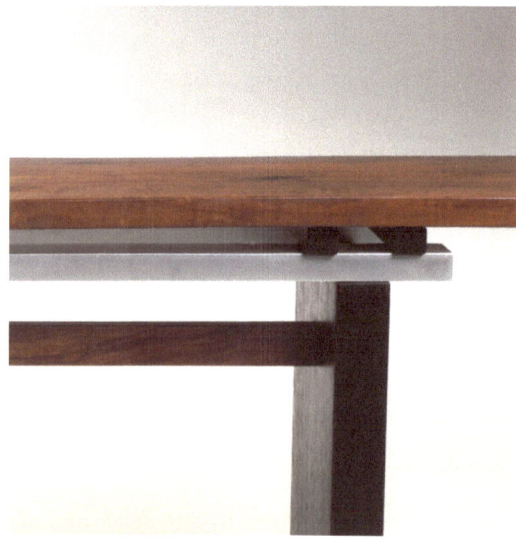

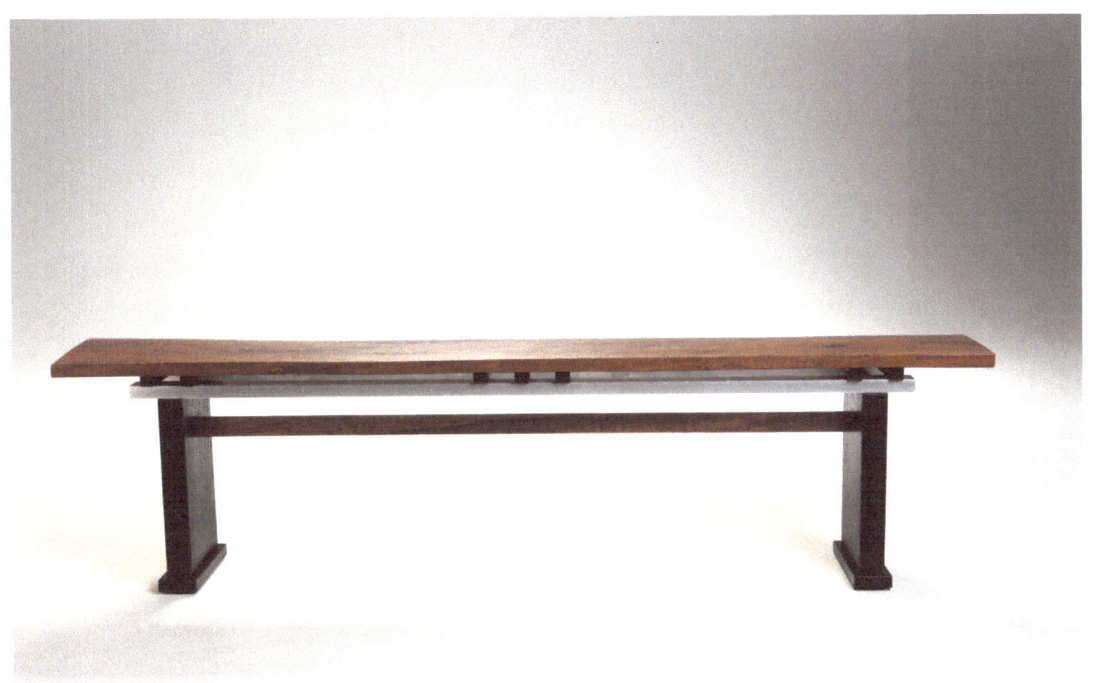

96H x 48W x 16D

Crafted of Birch, Poplar, Walnut, and PaperStone
2014

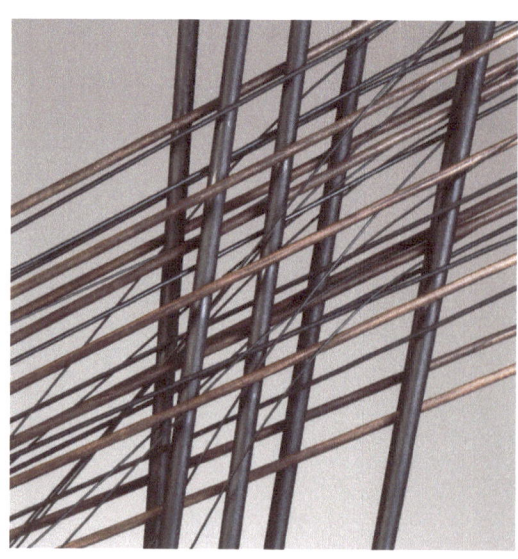

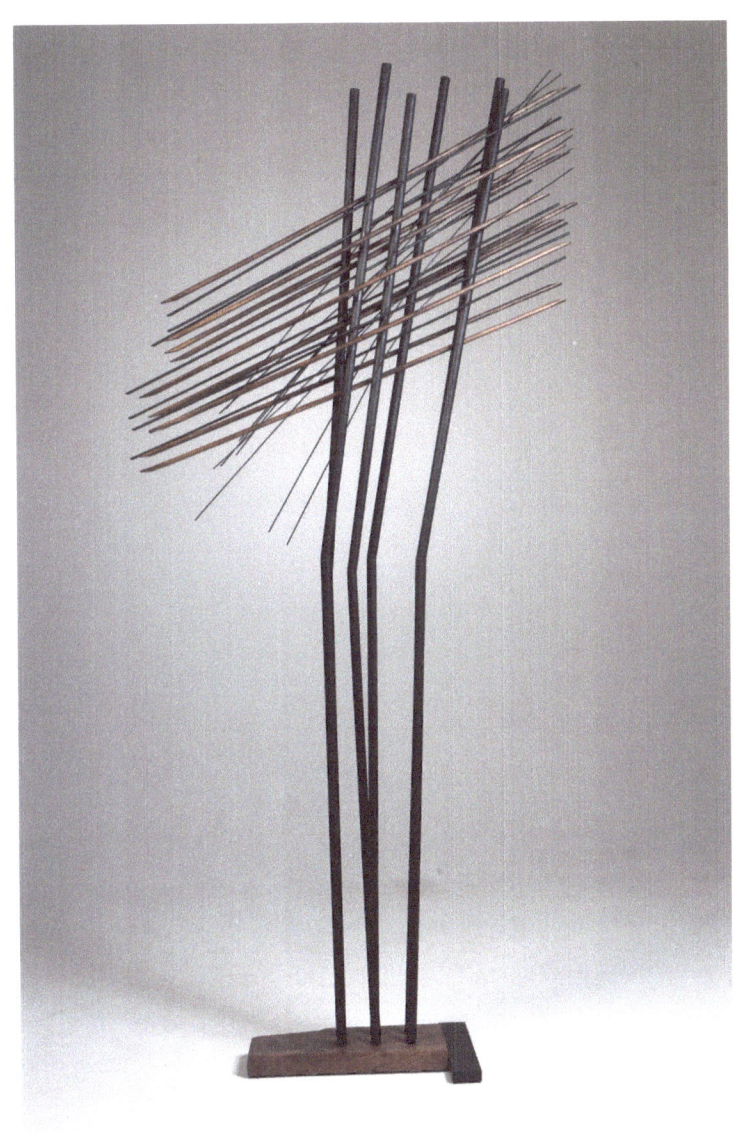

70H X 174W X 7D

Crafted of Jatoba, Maple, and Synskin
2011

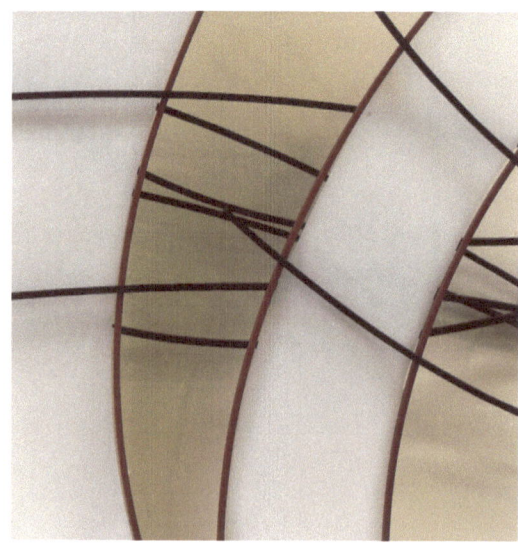

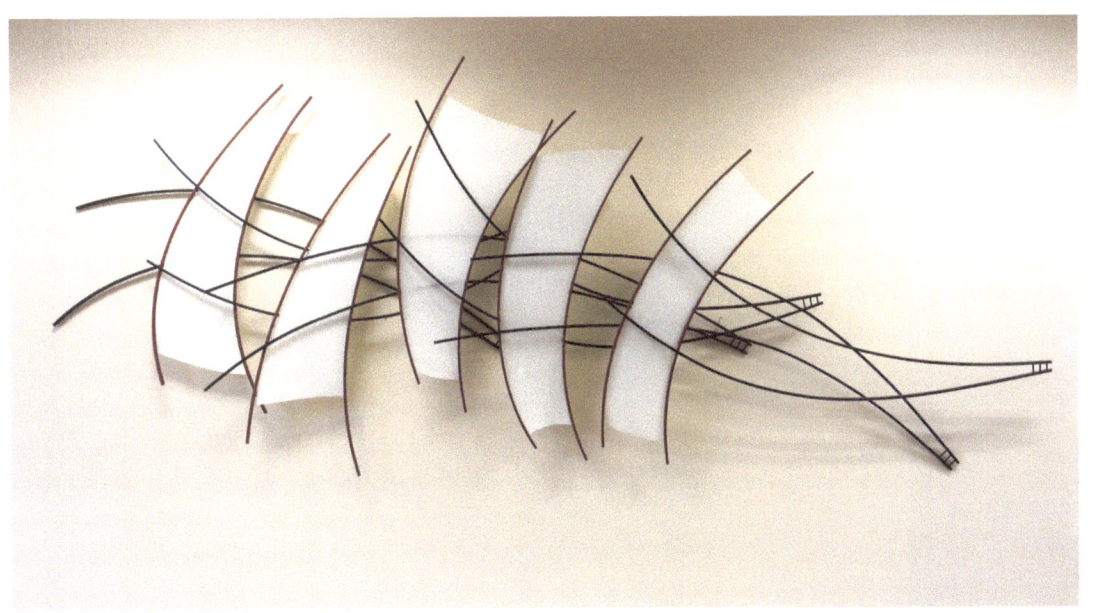

RIDING THE WIND II

REFLECTIONS ON THE WORK

I am always asked questions about my work like: *Where do your ideas come from? Do you have a specific idea in mind for each piece you build? Do you draw plans before you start working?* The simple answers are: *I don't know, no, and no.* As with most artist's statements, the following comments are after-the-fact reflections. I think that my work is more the result of a process, rather than a plan. I usually work only with the materials that I have on hand and I am always preparing the parts that I will be using in the future. I have no specific plan for these parts but consider them to be a palette to choose from, much like a painter has tubes of paint on hand for use. I start a project by looking at the available parts, then begin to arrange and assemble the pieces.

The finished pieces are rarely planned in advance. Any apparent influences shown in the work are less intentional than incidental to the process. I am evaluating each piece as I work, making choices that are informed by my experiences and likes, and sense of balance and proportion. I adjust and rearrange the parts until things start to gel, and quit when I feel that the work has developed into a coherent whole.

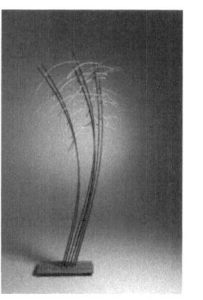

CASCADE

I started forming this piece in my mind while looking at a pile of parts: six long walnut arches and a handful of smaller arced pieces. My decision to use the longer pieces vertically started the process that determined how this piece evolved. I attached the smaller arched pieces horizontally and began to feel that the overall look resembled the form of trees and how they move in a breeze. This isn't meant to be a literal representation of a grove of trees, but I think it does create the same sense of flow and calmness.

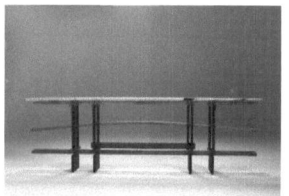

PAGODA TABLE

I have built a series of long narrow tables over the years, usually starting with a piece of wood that seemed to be perfect for a top and then designing a base that I felt complemented the shape of that piece. In this case the top had an irregular shape, so I created a symmetrical base both to enhance its form and to contrast with its natural edges. I wanted the overall appearance to be very open, so I shifted the visual mass of the piece to the base to maintain a sense of lightness. The look of the finished piece reflects my fondness of Japanese architecture and timber frame construction. This is reinforced by the contrast between the arch and the straight line horizontal and vertical pieces.

This is part of a series of pieces inspired by the increasing availability of new architectural products manufactured from recycled materials. The beauty of these stone-like materials suggested to me the possibilities of their use in creating minimalistic sculptural work. I used subtly shaped sculptural elements which, while thin when seen on edge, take on a sense of mass when light plays across their wider surfaces. This piece depends as much on the empty space between the two elements as it does on their respective shapes to create the overall impact of the finished work.

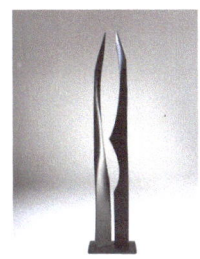

GEOMETRIC TANGO

I have always loved the look of bamboo when green and in full growth and also the look of the dried canes. Since it grows in our yard, I not only can observe and enjoy it but I have a ready source of material. With this piece I tried to give a sense of how bamboo clusters grow and how the shadows and light play between the shoots as they sway in a breeze. The feeling of this play of light against dark in this piece is constrained within the boundaries of its columnar form and the shadows that it casts.

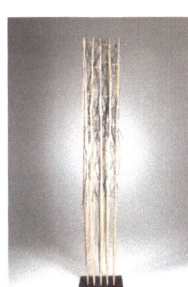

BAMBOO GROOVE

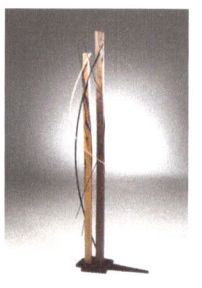

This piece was constructed from two twisted and split pieces of wood that would usually have been thrown onto the scrap pile. I found their unique shapes beautiful so I let these pieces play against each other with just a few added curved connections. The contrasting angled base gives the composition a sense of both lightness and direction.

ANGLES AND ARCS

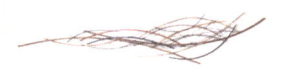

I was working with large arches on this piece and felt that it was important to create a sense of flow and direction to prevent it from appearing overly bulky. There is a balance between openness and density in this piece with the result seeming to evoke the motion of water flowing over rocks.

RAPIDS

This is part of a series that I always intended to be both simple and fun. The basic premise is to create a piece that while static, seems to be caught at the brink of collapse. The pure geometry of the elements comprising this piece, with no shaping or softening of their contours, helps reinforce the sense of a precarious situation.

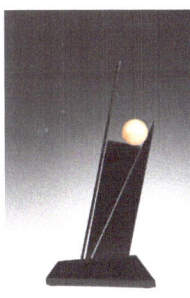

BALANCING ACT

I was working with a new composite material, Kirei, which, when banded with a black border, reminded me of tatami mats. This brought traditional Japanese architecture to mind, so I built the frame and base in a way that reflected the timber frame construction techniques that these buildings traditionally use. I staggered the frame elements and skewed the top panels to break up the otherwise formal regularity of this piece.

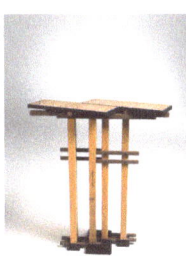

ZIG ZAG TABLE

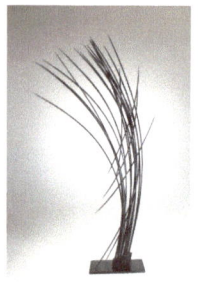

LARGE VERTICAL
ARC

I have been experimenting with an approach that I think of as 3-D sketching, sculpting with black narrow pieces which, in effect, look like inked lines drawn in the air. I wanted to emphasize the line elements rather than the volume of the piece: the image of arcs suspended in space. The openness of the piece helps emphasis a sense of movement.

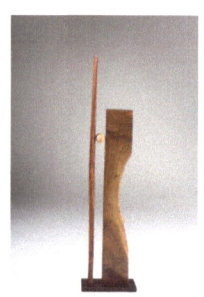

ABSTRACTION

This is constructed simply from one shaped piece, one natural edged piece, and a wooden ball. I was aiming for a sense of elegant calm; hence, there is no elaboration of the basic form. The beauty of the wood was allowed to stand on its own. Sometimes less is more.

This is one of a long series of tables which share in common the basic characteristic of a narrow cantilevered top supported by a center column. This piece departs from the others in that the top is extremely irregular in shape. Much longer braces support the top piece. I added asymmetric details to the base to create a sense of non-regular formality while complementing the natural shape of the top.

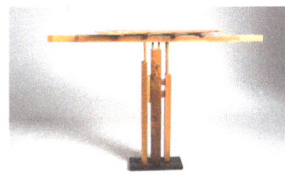

SAMURAI TABLE

This piece is constructed from very few elements. I find it a challenge to create a large, minimally styled piece that seems to occupy space without either looking stretched or underdeveloped. The open borders help to visually expand the composition without adding weight, yet still allow it to feel complete.

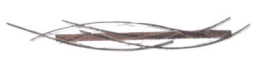

ARC FORM

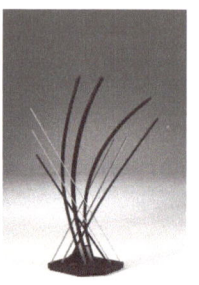

ANGULAR
MOMENTUM

This piece was conceived as a pure exercise in geometry. I had no specifics in mind except the play of curves against straight lines. The contrast of materials adds an additional sense of depth and emphasizes the variations of changing light and shadow. The result does seem to generate a sense of ongoing movement.

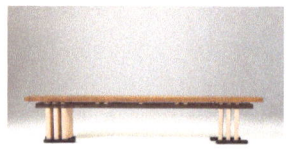

SLANTED BENCH

When I build benches I always start with the finished slab of wood to use for the top. The design of the base details depends on the shape and grain pattern of that top piece. In this case, I was starting with a beautiful rectangular piece of cherry. I felt that a formal design would complement the regularity of the top. I used slanted base panels and staggered foot elements to add a sense of liveliness to what otherwise would have been a static composition.

I love minimalism—in this case the composition is comprised of only a rock and two wooden ribbons. I wanted to create a sense of both solidity and airiness by contrasting the stone mass with sweeping vertical forms. The vertical sweep of these elements extends the scale of the piece beyond its size.

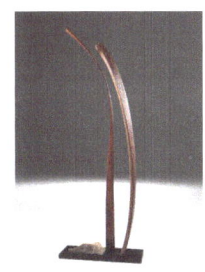

EARTH BELOW,
SKY ABOVE

I have always been interested in structural forms such as bridges or building frames. This piece plays off that interest, and despite its sense of irregularity is actually a formal work. The slanted lines and contrasting curved pieces serve to create a sense of the tension and imbalance that seems implicit in the action of taking a step forward.

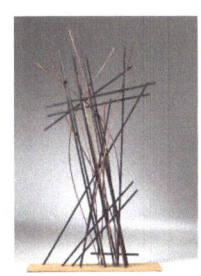

WALKING
LATTICE

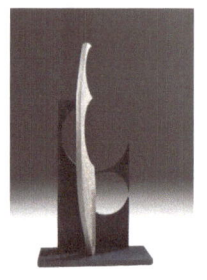

GEOMETRIC
TANGO

This piece is another exercise in pure geometry—a contrast of light and dark forms. The open spaces in this piece are almost as large as the elements that comprise it. This negative space lightens the sense of mass inherent in the stone-like materials that shape the work.

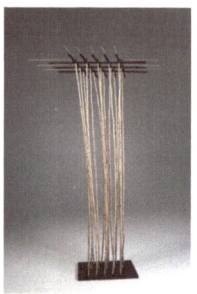

SKY GRID

The form of this piece is defined by the contrast between the irregularity implicit in bamboo canes, and the formal regularity of the base and grid work that crowns the top. The variation of light and dark between these elements enhances the sense of informality that this otherwise formal piece displays.

This is one of the few pieces that was directly inspired by a specific source: in this case photographs in a book on Japanese kites. I was fascinated by their sail-like shapes and wanted to capture that feeling of flying. The slenderness of the vertical lines helps to create the sense that the top elements are actually floating in the air.

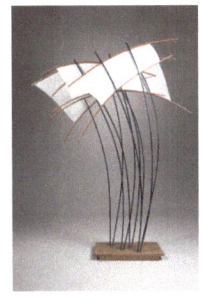

RIDING THE
WIND I

This is a very formal piece, designed with what I think of as balanced asymmetry. The intersections between the linear forms and the curved elements help create a sense of tension. This tension and the contrast of the colors of the various woods gives the piece a dynamic feel, yet the piece still exhibits a sense of calm.

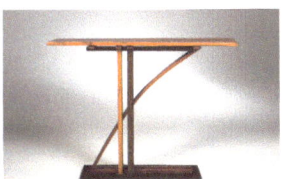

Z TABLE

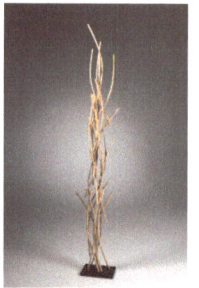

2 X 4   24

This piece had its origins in a traditional woodworking club challenge: start with a standard lumber yard 8 foot long 2 x 4, and, using no extra wood, make something with it. I chose to make a sculpture out of 24 matching arcs woven together. The result seemed to give the feeling either of rising flames or of falling water, and seems to belie its humble origins.

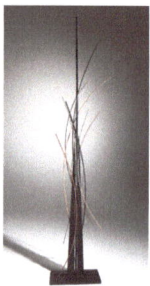

SILHOUETTE

As a starting point I used a couple of elongated angular forms mounted vertically, then added contrasting arched elements. The black foundation elements almost recede into shadow, while the various colored arch elements are highlighted by comparison. Depending on the viewing angle, this piece can seem either massive or very light.

This series of work is based on the contrast between naturally shaped pieces of wood and pieces of wood that I have shaped. The intersecting narrow arched elements highlight the natural wood shapes, and by comparison seem almost grass-like. Much like some styles of Japanese gardens, this manipulated form creates the sense of viewing an enhanced natural landscape.

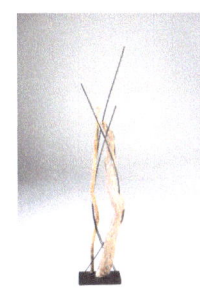

PRAIRIE
ABSTRACTION

This is one of a series of minimalist works that I have created, usually constructed from only two vertical elements. The subtle shape of these elements and their orientation defines the negative space between them. How well this relationship works can make or break the finished work in a piece this simple in composition. There is no elaboration of form beyond what is necessary.

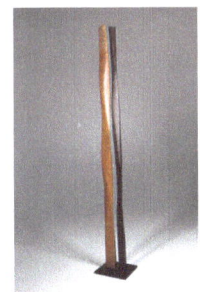

GRACIOUS DUO

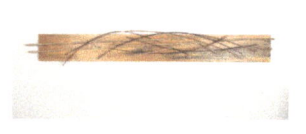

BAMBOO PANEL

Most of the wall pieces I construct are completely open designs with no apparent defined borders. I wanted to think of this piece as more of a painting with the background panel serving as a type of frame. This panel occupies space in a much different way than open frame pieces do, with the solid background adding a sense of weight that more open designs lack.

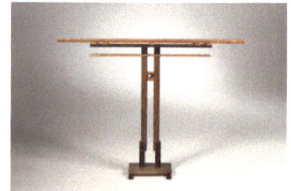

SAMURAI TABLE

This piece retains the basic format of this series—the cantilevered top, but with a more deconstructed base design. I wanted to keep the formal balance of elements within this piece while using the staggered column design and natural center brace to enliven the composition.

This was one of the first large Tango pieces that I constructed, keeping in mind that the scale and type of material used permit this piece be placed outside rather than be limited to indoor display. The larger scale of this simple composition makes the shaping of the elements and the space between them more apparent than in a smaller piece. Because of the size, there is a far wider viewing range to consider. This scale and the work's apparent mass gives this piece a strong visual presence—almost architectural in its effect.

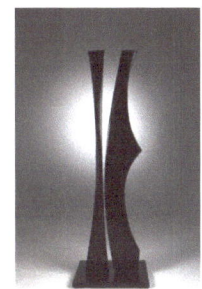

GEOMETRIC
TANGO

This piece is a departure from most sculptures that I have done in that it is comprised entirely of curved elements. The flow of these pieces creates a sense of movement with no obvious boundary. The different colors of the various woods helps enhance the sense of depth and dimension in the finished work.

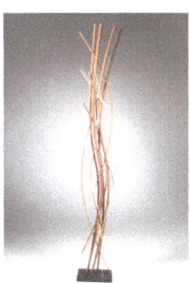

RHYTHM

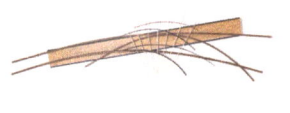

ANGLE WALL

Earlier I had banded a section of bamboo panel which then formed the foundation of this piece. After playing with the arrangement of the arched elements I then decided that aligning the piece at an angle would be a good starting point. The addition of a fan-like series of line elements gave it an almost traditional Japanese look. This is a large piece, but it has a surprisingly light look.

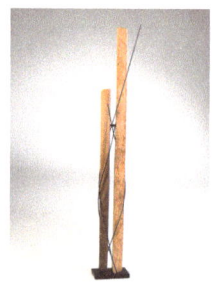

ABSTRACT

I started with two unique pieces of wood: one retaining the natural live edge, the other subtly shaped. Minimal elaboration of these components seemed to be the proper approach to take with this piece. It resembles the prairie pieces that I have done but is simpler in form: the contrast between the two main elements defining the work.

This piece is the first of my works where I experimented with the concept of 3-D drawing, letting the arched pieces stand in for lines of ink on paper. It is also one of the few pieces inspired by other images: in this case Hokusai's classic print *The Great Wave off Kanagawa*. I find the magnified, almost still image of the wave details in this print to be fascinating, and wanted to create that same feeling in a defined open-air space. There is a strong sense of arrested movement in this piece, yet a calmness at the same time.

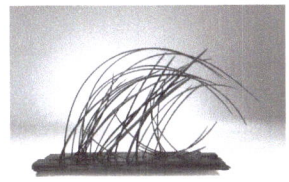

THE WAVE

The piece of wood that I chose for this table was very highly figured, so I felt that keeping the structure simple would be appropriate. This is a much more contemporary design than most of the tables I've built. The arch isn't structural, but it provides a necessary defining of the space between the vertical supports. This minimalism gives the table an elegantly simple composition.

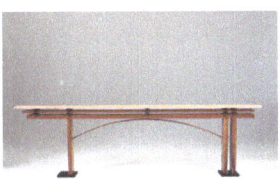

ARC TABLE

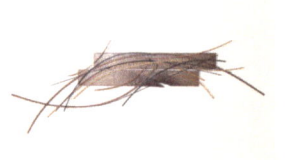

STEP

This is a commissioned piece, intended to be installed above a stairwell. I arranged the back panels to reflect this placement, and added the curved elements to convey the sense of movement from level to level.

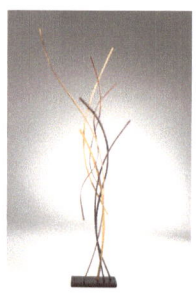

RHYTHM

This piece is intended to convey a sense of movement through the use of only curved elements. Its composition is pared back to as few elements as possible to reinforce this feeling without feeling cluttered. Even with its very minimal design this piece seems to embrace a larger volume of space than its size would indicate.

This is the simplest piece that I've constructed in this series. I started with a piece of walnut which still had a live edge and wove just three curved elements around it. These grass-like elements seem to have grown in place rather than placed as the result of the construction process.

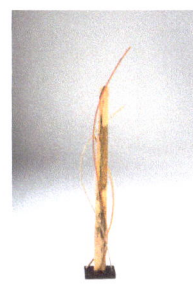

PRAIRIE
ABSTRACTION

This table is an elaboration on the Samurai Table series, in that it retains the narrow cantilevered top. The grid design of the column is reflected in the base and these two elements together give the piece an almost a Mondrian-like appearance. Despite its complex construction this piece retains a sense of simplicity of composition.

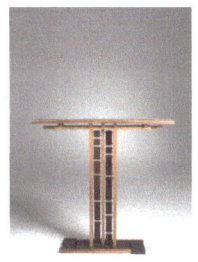

GRID TABLE

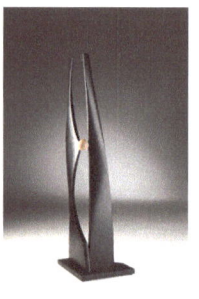

GEOMETRIC
TANGO

The success of a piece this minimal places great importance on the beauty of the materials used. The main elements are softly contoured, with the suspended ball barely seeming to be held in place. The luster of the materials and the contrast of color and form enhance the play of light across the piece and strengthen the composition.

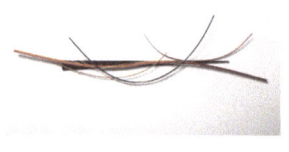

WEDGED ARC

This piece demonstrates an approach that I often employ: the contrast of curved and linear shapes. I employed a bare minimum of elements, but felt it important that the piece look complete. Its apparent size seems to extend beyond its borders, but it enlivens that space rather than dominates it.

This piece is comprised entirely by lines that seem to be drawn in the air. It almost seems to be a graphic representation of motion. Since the line elements taper, the boundaries appear to fade from view rather than define a specific space.

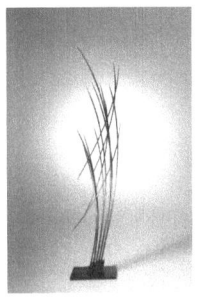

SMALL VERTICAL
ARC

I started with materials that seemed to demand a formal and straightforward approach be taken in its construction. When it was completed it looked like a contemporary interpretation of classic Japanese furniture design. It appears very elegant: composed of no more parts than what was required.

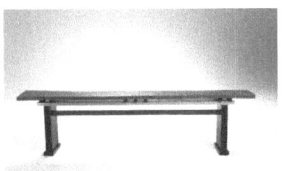

PAGODA BENCH

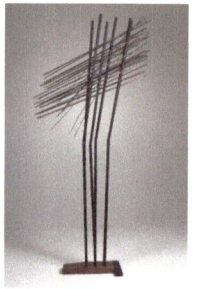

DARK SPECTRUM

This piece is an evolution of the sketch-like work that I have done previously. By using subtle color variations between the elements, the sense of depth and dimension was enhanced. The most distinguishing characteristic of this piece however, is its composition entirely from straight lines and angled pieces. This gives it a very directional, almost aggressive look.

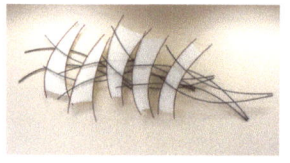

RIDING THE
WIND II

This, the second in the Wind series, is conceived as a wall piece rather than as a free-standing one. It has a more linear feel: the sense of depth maintained by the overlapping of the lines and panels. The lines are kept thin to enhance the sense of flying. The panels seem to float away from their anchor points.

CREDITS AND ACKNOWLEDGMENTS

I want to thank many people for their help in producing this portfolio.

All of the photography was done by Tom Sidebottom and David Van Allen and, with a couple of exceptions, all images were taken in David's studio. Thanks to David's incomparable ability to light the work, those images were more revelatory of the pieces than anything I had expected.

Tom did most of the hard work when it came to entering data, page layout and editing, all of which made my ideas and information readable and sensible. I knew how I wanted the basic portfolio to be arranged and what information I wanted to convey, but he made it happen.

I have worked with Sean Ulmer for many years on a number of projects. He knows my work intimately. I thank him for taking the time to assemble the analysis of my work that opens this book.

I wanted the look of the completed book to complement the design of my first portfolio which was designed by Bill Basler. I hope that we lived up to the standard that he set.

I also need to thank all of the gallery owners and museum personnel that I have worked with over the years. They host the shows; display and place my work; keep it in the public eye.

Many should be thanked for having to put up with me dragging them into the shop to look at and critique the latest piece, something that I find very helpful.

And last but not least, I thank my clients and patrons who have purchased my work. Without their support this would still be a hobby.

www.ingramcontent.com/pod-product-compliance
Lightning Source LLC
Chambersburg PA
CBHW050721180526
45159CB00003B/1093